Set design by Tony Straiges   Costume design by Martin Pakledinaz   Photo by T. Charles Erickson

A scene from the Hartford Stage production of *The Learned Ladies of Park Avenue*.

THE LEARNED LADIES OF PARK AVENUE

BY DAVID GRIMM

TRANSLATED AND FREELY ADAPTED
FROM MOLIÈRE'S *LES FEMMES SAVANTES*

DRAMATISTS
PLAY SERVICE
INC.

THE LEARNED LADIES OF PARK AVENUE
Copyright © 2006, David Grimm

All Rights Reserved

CAUTION: Professionals and amateurs are hereby warned that performance of THE LEARNED LADIES OF PARK AVENUE is subject to payment of a royalty. It is fully protected under the copyright laws of the United States of America, and of all countries covered by the International Copyright Union (including the Dominion of Canada and the rest of the British Commonwealth), and of all countries covered by the Pan-American Copyright Convention, the Universal Copyright Convention, the Berne Convention, and of all countries with which the United States has reciprocal copyright relations. All rights, including professional/amateur stage rights, motion picture, recitation, lecturing, public reading, radio broadcasting, television, video or sound recording, all other forms of mechanical or electronic reproduction, such as CD-ROM, CD-I, DVD, information storage and retrieval systems and photocopying, and the rights of translation into foreign languages, are strictly reserved. Particular emphasis is placed upon the matter of readings, permission for which must be secured from the Author's agent in writing.

The English language stock and amateur stage performance rights in the United States, its territories, possessions and Canada for THE LEARNED LADIES OF PARK AVENUE are controlled exclusively by DRAMATISTS PLAY SERVICE, INC., 440 Park Avenue South, New York, NY 10016. No professional or nonprofessional performance of the Play may be given without obtaining in advance the written permission of DRAMATISTS PLAY SERVICE, INC., and paying the requisite fee.

Inquiries concerning all other rights should be addressed to International Creative Management, Inc., 40 West 57th Street, New York, NY 10019. Attn: Patrick Herold.

SPECIAL NOTE

Anyone receiving permission to produce THE LEARNED LADIES OF PARK AVENUE is required to give credit to the Author as sole and exclusive Author of the Play on the title page of all programs distributed in connection with performances of the Play and in all instances in which the title of the Play appears for purposes of advertising, publicizing or otherwise exploiting the Play and/or a production thereof. The name of the Author must appear on a separate line, in which no other name appears, immediately beneath the title and in size of type equal to 50% of the size of the largest, most prominent letter used for the title of the Play. No person, firm or entity may receive credit larger or more prominent than that accorded the Author. The following acknowledgment must appear on the title page in all programs distributed in connection with performances of the Play:

Commissioned and originally produced
by Hartford Stage Company.

*To Michael Wilson,
with my thanks*

THE LEARNED LADIES OF PARK AVENUE premiered at Hartford Stage, in Hartford, Connecticut, on September 1, 2005. It was directed by Michael Wilson; the set design was by Tony Straiges; the costume design was by Martin Pakledinaz; the lighting design was by Rui Rita; the original music and sound design were by John Gromada; and the production stage manager was Carmelita Becnel. The cast was as follows:

HENRY CRYSTAL	Tom Bloom
PHYLLIS CRYSTAL	Annalee Jefferies
RAMONA	Nancy Bell
BETTY	Nicole Lowrance
UNCLE RUPERT	Nafe Katter
AUNT SYLVIA	Pamela Payton-Wright
DICKY MAYHEW	Zach Shaffer
UPTON GABBITT	David Greenspan
MAGDA	Natalie Brown
T.S. BAINS, JUDGE ARBOGAST	Bill Kux
SERVANTS	Elizabeth Capinera, Dan Whelton

CHARACTERS

HENRY CRYSTAL, a well-to-do businessman

PHYLLIS CRYSTAL, his wife

RAMONA, their eldest daughter

BETTY, their younger daughter

UNCLE RUPERT, Henry's brother

AUNT SYLVIA, Henry's sister

DICKY MAYHEW, Betty's beau

UPTON GABBITT, a writer

MAGDA, a Hungarian cook

T. S. BAINS, a writer

JUDGE ARBOGAST, may be doubled by the actor playing Bains

PLACE

Park Avenue, New York City.

TIME

1936.

THE LEARNED LADIES OF PARK AVENUE

ACT ONE

Scene 1

Mid-morning. The radio is playing some jazzy number. Betty enters, dancing. Ramona enters and switches it off. Betty shows off her ring.

RAMONA.
What? Tell me you're ribbing, Sis, say it's a joke!
BETTY.
No —
RAMONA.
    You'd ditch being daughter and take on the yoke
Of the title of "Missus" — Or worse yet, "My Wife"?
BETTY.
We —
RAMONA.
    I'd sooner poke out both my eyes with a knife!
BETTY.
What's so wrong about marriage? It's —
RAMONA.
                            — Give me a break!
Were you born in a barn?
BETTY.
              —No but —
RAMONA.
                          — Oh, for Pete's sake!

The whole concept's absurd! Say it: "Marriage" — You see?
Sounds like a disease! Betty, take it from me,
I'm sure it's quite jolly for shopgirls from Queens
Or Brooklyn or Staten — Poor slobs without means
Who can't make good choices and don't know what's what;
But young ladies like us can't be tying the knot.
Having brats, getting fat — Oh, and running a house —
And spending each day as the slave of your spouse —
Why, the thought makes me sick! The results are obscene!
Are you out of your mind?
BETTY.
                         Not at all. I'm quite keen.
Getting married's the subject of all young girls' dreams —
The dress and the trousseaux, the cake, and the screams
Of the bridesmaids who jockey to catch the bouquet,
The rice that gets thrown, the champagne, and the way
Your fiancé looks as you walk down the aisle,
The folks who're so pleased that they cry as they smile;
But more than all that is the dream of uniting
Your life with the one that you love; how exciting!
What a wonderful future for him and for me.
Can't you see that, Ramona?
RAMONA.
                         Well, let me think — Gee!
Obeying and honoring all of his wishes,
And spending each night scrubbing grease off his dishes.
And keeping his shirt collars blindingly white,
Losing sleep 'cause he snores like a bear every night;
Forcing laughter at jokes when you just want to groan,
And adopting his tastes and ideas as your own:
His lectures on baseball and how to save money,
Why Jimmy Durante is actually funny.
Is that the life, Betty, to which you'd aspire?
BETTY.
Oh stop it. You're not going to quash my desire,
Ramona.
RAMONA.
           Have you no higher hopes for your mind?
No ambitions to raise yourself out of the grind
Of everyday life with its mind-numbing muck?
Come on, wizen up, sister — You marry some cluck

And you may as well wash your whole life down the drain!
You don't see *me* with cow eyes! A life of the brain
Is what keeps me going — And look at our mother,
Who's erudite, savvy, and wise like no other.
From culture and art and the state of the union
To abstract philosophy, every opinion ·
She voices is widely respected and relished
For speaking of things as they are, unembellished.
So instead of this longing for animal lust,
You should follow her credo that "All flesh is dust,"
And in lieu of a marriage with husband and kid,
Seek a marriage of minds; you'll be glad that you did.
BETTY.
Our maker, Ramona, gives each their own course
To travel along to find joy or remorse.
We must be who we are and pursue our own lives
And be true to our natures as thinkers or wives.
We can both follow Mother's example in this,
Choosing paths of our own which will lead us to bliss;
You can emulate her through philosophy's might;
I, with husband and family. Please don't let's fight.
RAMONA.
If you emulate someone, sis, may I suggest
The behavior you copy from them is the best.
Things like poise and deportment and wisdom and wit;
You don't need to watch someone to learn how to spit.
BETTY.
If our mother had lived all her life for her mind
You and I wouldn't be here right now, so be kind.
RAMONA.
Just tell me this, Betty — The poor sucker who
You got marked for a chump isn't Dicky Mayhew.
BETTY.
And what if it is? What's so wrong about Dicky?
You can't really say that I haven't been picky
In choosing a possible mate?
RAMONA.
                          No, I couldn't.
Too picky, perhaps, 'cause a girl really shouldn't
Go stealing another gal's man like an outlaw
When everyone knows I'm the one that he pined for.

BETTY.
But you had no interest in him whatsoever!
The minute he'd talk about love, you would sever
All contact and rudely insist he grow up
And stop moping and sighing like some lovesick pup.
You always had loftier thoughts to consider
Than earthly desires; so please don't be bitter
If someone else takes up the heart you disdain
And offers it love and a shelter from pain.
RAMONA.
Betty, reason and logic should never imply
That I don't get a kick when I'm chased by a guy;
Just because I find marriage coarse, vulgar, and crude
Doesn't mean I don't like to be sought and pursued.
BETTY.
I would never prevent him from worshipping you;
And I only accepted him once you were through.
RAMONA.
Yes, but how can you say that you're perfectly sure
That his feelings for you are entirely pure?
What if all the attention he's giving you now
Is no more than a ploy to win me back somehow?
BETTY.
He swore on his soul that his love is the truth.
RAMONA.
Yeah, okay, but you're not some dumb hick from Duluth
Who believes any booshwa some fella can spout.
If Dick says he's over me, I really doubt
That he knows what he feels — It's just plain self-deceit.
BETTY.
I don't think so, Ramona.
(The doorbell sounds. A servant goes to answer the door. Dicky Mayhew is heard off stage: "Good morning! How's tricks?")
        But here's a concrete
Way of sorting the facts about whom he adores:
Here he comes. Let's go ask him and settle the scores.
(Dicky enters.)
DICKY.
Hiya, sprout, what's a-growin'? Ramona, what's new?
BETTY.
Dick, my sister and I have a question for you.

Please be brutally honest and bluntly impart
Which of us is the true love and girl of your heart?
RAMONA.
Oh please don't let's do this, it's terribly crass;
You embarrass him, Betty. Why not let it pass?
Declarations of love are a private affair
Not a public debate or a rude questionnaire.
DICKY.
No, Ramona, it's perfectly okay with me,
And I'll answer that question in all honesty.
See, apparently everything's just as you hoped.
For ages, your charms had my heart fairly roped;
My soul pledged to you its impassioned devotion
But yet your eyes gazed at me with no emotion.
I suffered in silence from your cold demeanor
And hoped it would change, but you only grew meaner
With every attempt that I made to give pleasure.
At last, when I could not withstand one more measure
Of pain or rejection, I made up my mind
To love someone else who returns love in kind.
And that soul I found in the eyes of sweet Betty
Whose gentle devotion and love has been steady
As soft calming waves on the wide open ocean —
A far deeper joy than the endless commotion
Of heartbreak and misery which you provided.
She makes me feel happy and strong; I'm excited
To face any challenge that life may provide us;
And with her beside me, my heart's rich as Midas.
So Ramona, don't try to entice me away
'Cause it's useless; it's Betty I love and obey.
RAMONA.
Me? Entice you? That's rich! In a pig's valise, bub!
Why, you must have been struck in the head with a club!
BETTY.
Easy, sister, let's not be so rude or uncouth;
Where's the woman of reason, of logic, of truth?
Surely passion like anger's beneath you, my dear —
RAMONA.
I'm not rude or uncouth; as for anger — No fear!
But to hear the word truth on your lips is a joke
When you keep this whole matter clandestine and cloak

It in secrecy from those whose blessing you need.
BETTY.
What?
RAMONA.
   Without Mom's permission, you'll never succeed.
So don't talk about reason or logic with me
When instead you should get down on your bended knee
And pray she approves of your choice in a mate.
Don't go betting on horses that ain't at the gate.
BETTY.
She's right, of course, Dicky: I haven't been honest
With Mother or Father; I shouldn't have promised
My hand without first seeking out their approval.
If we don't do that, Dick, they'll seek your removal
And find someone else whom they'll want me to marry.
RAMONA.
Our mother's tough stubbornness is legendary.
BETTY.
You must talk to them and, perhaps by confessing
Your feelings for me, they might grant us their blessing.
DICKY.
'Course I'll talk to them, pal. I'll do all that it takes
To have you as my bride. Heck, I'd even charm snakes!
RAMONA.
So you win, little Betty. You think I'm upset?
BETTY.
Not at all, my dear sister. I'm deep in your debt
For your strong sense of duty and canny advice.
Your innate grasp of logic is always precise,
Which is why you must rescue us! Please intercede
And appeal on our part 'til our folks are agreed
They should let us get married — Oh, say that you will!
RAMONA.
Betty, sometimes, you know, you can be such a pill —
Going on about marriage and shouldn'ts and shoulds
When the heart that you long for is secondhand goods.
BETTY.
Secondhand it may be, but you cannot deny
If you thought you could take it back from me, you'd try.
RAMONA.
I won't stoop to reply to a statement so crass.

It is best to let moments like this simply pass. *(Ramona exits.)*
BETTY.
Your confession has taken her quite by surprise.
DICKY.
Some folks only believe what's in front of their eyes.
Now come give me a kiss —
(They kiss.)

        — I'll talk to your father
And ask his permission —
BETTY.

         — You'd best start with Mother.
My father's a sweetie but his disposition
Is so mild and gentle; he'll give his permission,
And gladly at that — But he can't be relied on;
His determination's as sturdy as nylon.
He knows all one can about selling baked beans,
But he hasn't a clue what authority means.
He yields to whatever my mother desires
And at her objection, his purpose expires;
Whatever might please her is his raison d'etre.
She says the sky's green and I'm willing to betcha
He'll say it's green too and he'll give in with grace
'Cause she calls all the shots and keeps him in his place.
So while it's a bore, you should try to enchant
And be kind, even flatter, my mother and aunt.
DICKY.
Look, it's not that I don't trust a woman who's wise,
In fact quite the reverse, knowledge is quite a prize.
But a person whose only concern in this world
Is to be thought clever — Well, that's just absurd.
I'd rather hear someone say, "Gee, I don't know!"
Than put up with a pedant who spouts some bon mot,
Quoting authors or theories they don't understand
Thinking trite little platitudes give them command
To impress me with their breadth of knowledge. Well, heck!
I don't mean to be rude, but they're pains in the neck!
So although I respect your dear mother a lot
Her pretensions annoy me, as does that crackpot
Whom she venerates as the great mind of our day:
Upton Gabbitt's a fool and his writing's cliché —
Oh, it burns me right up to see all the respect

That she heaps on the head of that worthless insect
Whose books are so empty, the best he could wish
Is to hawk them on Fulton as wrapping for fish!
BETTY.
Yes, he and his books can be very annoying
And, like you, I find him exceedingly cloying;
But as he has influence over my mother
You really should try to find some way or other
To be, well, agreeable, not so defiant.
A lover must learn to be somewhat compliant
With those that his sweetheart is forced to endure
So that no one objects. Say you'll try? For me?
DICKY.
                                        Sure.
I'll do my best.
BETTY.
        Good.
DICKY.
                Boy, though, I just want to yip
When that Gabbitt starts in with his one-upmanship.
Heck, I can't even see straight when he's in the room.
Look, I don't want to spoil any chance as your groom,
But to compliment him or his books is too much!
I first read him before I had met him and such
A load of pretentious malarkey it was
That to meet him in person was shocking because
He's exactly as vapid as all of his work
Which proclaims social conscience while wearing the smirk
Of self-confident glee at how clever he is.
BETTY.
Gosh, you're really observant to notice all this.
DICKY.
He's a portrait of pride and of vein self-conceit,
Writing books about poor working men on the street
When he's never a day in his life had to face
Any hardship or breadlines or even the trace
Of privation or hunger, but sits lofty high
Handing down his pronouncements and theories on why
This Depression's the fault of those folks on relief.
Heck, I just want to haul off and sock 'im — Good grief!
(Sylvia can be heard offstage: "Help! For Christ's sake, would someone

... *Jesus!")*
Oh, but here comes your aunt. I should try to finesse
Her to talk to your mother so she'll acquiesce. *(They exchange a quick kiss. Betty exits. Sylvia enters, followed by servants carrying stacks of hatboxes.)*
SYLVIA.
If you ask me my version of "fate worse than death,"
It's a wop manicurist with terminal breath.
DICKY.
Hello, Sylvie. Been out shopping?
SYLVIA.
                              Be a sweetie,
Dicky dear, and mix me up a nice martini.
DICKY.
Very well. Say, I wonder if you have a few
Little moments to spare now to talk, me and you.
It's a delicate matter. A lover's distress.
SYLVIA.
Oh, not you as well, Dick. It's because of this dress.
Sure, my figure's a wonderful thing to behold
But in this I can't walk out without being told
I embody the beauty of Venus herself
(Which is boring as it often comes from an elf
With a hairlip, a walleye, and stains on his shirt).
But I hope you know better and don't start to flirt
Using all sorts of language to prove your deep love.
When I hear words of passion, I just want to shove
The poor man out a window — It's so very dull;
I prefer it when men keep their thoughts in their skull.
So adore me and love me, sigh deeply and pine,
And as long as you're silent, then everything's fine.
But if you should open your mouth to avow,
I'll be forced to insist that you leave here and now.
DICKY.
Oh I'm sorry there, Sylvie; you misunderstand.
It's Betty I cherish. I wish for her hand,
But I'm scared that my prospects aren't terribly good.
A kind word from you, though — That is, if you would —
SYLVIA.
Now that is one clever and subtle evasion
And worthy of high praise and congratulation.

In all of the novels that I have perused,
I've never once read of that ploy being used.
DICKY.
This isn't a ploy or a gag of some kind;
I'm telling you what's in my heart and my mind.
Fate has granted the unworthy soul of this boy
Such a beautiful gift that inspires hope and joy;
It makes my pulse race and my palms go all sweaty;
I never knew true love before meeting Betty.
Just thinking of her makes me brighten and smile.
More than anything I want to walk down the aisle
With her and through marriage, make our lives complete.
So I'll beg on my knees if you want and entreat
You to help us achieve this, 'cause my absolute
Future happiness hangs on my winning this suit.
SYLVIA.
Now Dick please, say no more; I'm not thick in the bean.
By using that name, I know just who you mean.
It's a very good code, and a smart metaphor,
So I'll give you my answer, but please don't be sore:
This "Betty" you mention is not keen on wedlock,
And if you pursue it, you'll find you're in deadlock.
It's better if you show your love and concern
Without ever expecting a thing in return.
DICKY.
Oh, Sylvia, why are you twisting this plot,
And insist on believing as true what is not?
SYLVIA.
Don't let's argue about this, and stop being grand.
You think I can't tell what's as plain as my hand?
You mustn't deny what your amorous look
Has conveyed to me, Dick. Your own face is a book
And the writing is clear. So why not let suffice
That I fathom your meaning. I'll try to be nice
And put up with your ardor and worship as long
As you remain decent and where you belong.
DICKY.
But —
SYLVIA.
    No! It's no use. I've said more than enough.
And if you don't like it — I'm sorry, that's tough.

DICKY.
But you got it all wrong!
SYLVIA.
                              What, you want me to blush?
My beautician says red doesn't suit me, so hush!
DICKY.
I would rather be horsewhipped than love you, I swear!
SYLVIA.
Then quit following me like some dog everywhere!
(Sylvia exits.)
DICKY.
Like some dog? Follow you? Are you hopped up on dope?
I thought she would help us. Apparently, nope!
Her head is so full of delusions and folly —
I've never seen anything like it. But golly,
I won't let this setback destroy my campaign.
I'll find someone else here to help — Someone sane!

End of Act One

ACT TWO

Late morning. Uncle Rupert and Dicky by the open front door.

DICKY.
See —
RUPERT.
    I understand, Dick.
DICKY.
                      She —
RUPERT.
                            I'm sure.
DICKY.
                                  I —
RUPERT.
                                      No doubt.
DICKY.
Will —
RUPERT.
    Of course I will help you. There's no need to shout.
DICKY.
But —
RUPERT.
    I'll talk to them, Dick.
DICKY.
                          They —
RUPERT.
                                  I'll do all I can.
DICKY.
Thanks! I must get to work.
(Dicky exits.)
RUPERT.
                        Boy, he talks — man, oh man!
Whether happy, morose, on a cloud, in a huff,
Folks in love use ten words when just one is enough!
(Henry Crystal enters with the morning papers.)

HENRY.
(Singing to himself.)
Beans, beans, the musical fruit,
The more you eat, the more you toot;
The more you toot, the better you feel,
So have some beans with every meal.
RUPERT.
Brother Henry! How's business? Beans selling okay?
HENRY.
"A day without beans ain't a regular day."
Do you like that? It's catchy. My newspaper ad.
Why the face? Oh no, Rupert. Don't tell me it's bad.
RUPERT.
Do you know why I'm here?
HENRY.
                    I'm about to find out.
RUPERT.
You've known Dick a long time.
HENRY.
                           Dick? Since he was a sprout.
He visits us often and he's always welcome.
RUPERT.
He's quite a sharp kid; bright, considerate, handsome —
HENRY.
His old man and I, we were roommates at Yale —
RUPERT.
So I've heard.
HENRY.
          A good friend and an athlete most hale.
RUPERT.
So you've said.
HENRY.
            We were mere lads back then, but as pals —
Oh, the pranks we got up to while chasing the gals!
One time we went out for some drinks with this vamp
And ended up dressed in her clothes.
RUPERT.
                        Oh how camp!
But Henry, enough of this nostalgic chatter;
Allow me to get to the heart of the matter:
(Sylvia enters, unnoticed.)

Dicky has asked me to test out the water
And tell you he's fallen for Betty, your daughter.
HENRY.
What? With Betty?
RUPERT.
      He's told me at length how he feels,
And it's clear to me, brother, he's head over heels.
SYLVIA.
You must have heard wrong, Rupert;
That's a mistake. It's somebody else who makes Dicky's heart ache.
RUPERT.
Dicky loves someone other than Betty? No sir.
SYLVIA.
I would bet bottom dollar.
RUPERT.
      He swore it was her!
SYLVIA.
But of course he would do that.
RUPERT.
        And that's why I say,
That it's on Dick's behalf that I've come here today.
SYLVIA.
And your point?
RUPERT.
    He's too nervous to do as he planned,
So he asked me to ask you to grant him her hand.
SYLVIA.
Now that's clever! He couldn't have thought of a ruse
That's more gallant and charming. But just *entre-nous*,
Using Betty's a pretext, a screen, a charade,
A device to keep his true desire in the shade.
RUPERT.
Sister, since you appear to have details galore,
Why not tell us the truth? Whom does Dicky adore?
SYLVIA.
I'm not sure I should spill.
RUPERT.
      Come now, Sylvia. Tell!
SYLVIA.
Very well. It is I.

RUPERT.
                    You?
SYLVIA.
                            Yes.
RUPERT.
                                    Ho, ho — Like hell!
SYLVIA.
What exactly does that exclamation portend?
Is it really so shocking? Can't you comprehend
That men find me alluring, desirable, sweet?
Why, they try every day to sweep me off my feet!
Chuckie, Bill, Lawrence, Desmond, Frank, Harry, and Paul,
Oh, the list is so long, I can hardly name all.
RUPERT.
You say those men love you?
SYLVIA.
                            Yes, in spirit and flesh.
RUPERT.
Have they told you as much?
SYLVIA.
                                What, and let them get fresh?
They have shown wise restraint and their deepest respect,
Never letting their lust to run rampant, unchecked.
RUPERT.
We never see Desmond or Bill come to visit.
SYLVIA.
Because their regard for me is so exquisite.
RUPERT.
Whenever Paul sees you, he rattles his cage.
SYLVIA.
That's just what you get with such hot jealous rage.
RUPERT.
Chuck, Harry, and Frank are all happily wed.
SYLVIA.
My rejection of them made them wish themselves dead.
RUPERT.
As for Lawrence, he's selling antiques now, I hear.
SYLVIA.
Some poor saps who can't have me just up and go queer.
RUPERT.
Well, it's plain you don't suffer from low self-esteem.

HENRY.
Don't you think it's time, sister, you woke from these dreams?
SYLVIA.
Dreams, you call them? What, me? I have dreams? Oh, that's rich!
All this time I thought facts were the truth — What a switch!
Henry, you make me laugh. Well, hot dog, I have dreams!
Wait till I go tell Phyllis, she'll bust at the seams!
(Sylvia exits, laughing.)
HENRY.
Our sister's insane.
RUPERT.
              It gets worse every day.
But back to my point now that Miss Thing is away.
Dick asks your permission to marry young Betty;
Can I say you'll give him your blessing already?
HENRY.
Do you have to ask? I mean, isn't it clear?
If Betty loves Dick, he's got nothing to fear.
RUPERT.
You know that he's not that secure or well-off —
HENRY.
These days, well, who is? That's no reason to scoff.
He's wealthy in other ways far more important,
Which gives him, to my mind, an instant preferment.
So what if he is just a low mailroom clerk?
He's smart, he's ambitious, he's not scared to work.
Besides which, his dear dad and I were such chums,
I know he'd agree, it's the best of outcomes.
RUPERT.
Then let's go see Phyllis, your wife, and make good.
HENRY.
There's no reason to, Rupert. I said that they could.
RUPERT.
Yes, but Henry, don't you think the mom of the bride
Has a say in this matter to help you decide?
HENRY.
Oh Rupert, you really are one funny guy.
If you think she could change my mind, spit in my eye.
RUPERT.
There's spit in your eye.

HENRY.
                    Look, just leave it to me, bub.
I'll break it to her and there won't be no hubbub.
RUPERT.
Very well. And I'll go talk to Betty and find
Out how she's keeping up.
HENRY.
                         Yes, well, I know my mind,
And my wife will obey me and do as she's told.
(Rupert exits. Magda enters, crying.)
MAGDA.
Mit csináltam? Is not true, that saying of old
That is better to serve in the heaven than reign
Down in hell.
HENRY.
              Magda, what's wrong? Why do you complain?
MAGDA.
Me? Complain? Ha! Madame she just tell me to burn.
HENRY.
To burn?
MAGDA.
        I mean, she fire me so I can't earn
The small money she pay me to cook all your food.
HENRY.
She fired you? What? No, she's just in a mood.
You know how she sometimes gets short with her temper,
But you're a good cook, Magda. No, please, don't whimper.
As head of this house, I say you keep your job.
(Phyllis enters, followed by Sylvia.)
PHYLLIS.
What, are you still here, you Hungarian slob?
Thief, get out of my house! Never more show your face!
HENRY.
Phyllis —
PHYLLIS.
          No, it's enough!
HENRY.
                          But —
PHYLLIS.
                                She's ruined, debased
A fine home with her squalor!

HENRY.
> But what has she done?

PHYLLIS.
Do you dare take her side, that malodorous Hun?

HENRY.
No, I only was asking —

PHYLLIS.
> It's like a cabal!

Sylvie, see how they try to destroy my morale?

HENRY.
Phyllis, I only asked you to tell me her crime.

PHYLLIS.
Henry, why do you doubt my intent all the time?
Have I ever dismissed someone without just cause?

HENRY.
I didn't say that now; I'm sure she has flaws —

PHYLLIS.
Flaws, you call them? A criminal mind, nothing less!
I will not have such riffraff befoul this address.
Now either you show her the door and *adieu,*
Or —

HENRY.
> No, no; I'm sure what you say is quite true.

PHYLLIS.
I won't stand to be argued with in my own home.

HENRY.
Yes.

PHYLLIS.
> If you were a husband instead of a gnome,

You'd share in my outrage and show indignation.

HENRY.
Yes, Magda, you'd best let this job termination
Serve as a good lesson; this isn't your calling.
My wife is quite right, 'cause your crime is appalling.

MAGDA.
But what have I done?

HENRY.
> Heck, search me — I don't know!

PHYLLIS.
Still proclaiming her innocence? Tell her to go!

HENRY.
Did she break your fine china or chip a wineglass?
PHYLLIS.
Do you think I'd dismiss her for that? You're a gas.
HENRY.
Has she stolen or ruined a priceless heirloom?
PHYLLIS.
Trifling piffle like that wouldn't spell out her doom.
HENRY.
Did she murder the dog and then dance a *czardas?*
PHYLLIS.
Would I ever take action on something so rash?
HENRY.
Then what in Grant's tomb could be so darn perverse
That she has to be fired?
PHYLLIS.
              Oh, Henry, it's worse.
HENRY.
Worse than all of these things?
PHYLLIS.
                It's like hell's own abyss!
HENRY.
Oh my God, did she season the soup with her —
PHYLLIS.
                          This
Is her crime, her misdeed, her most lawless offense!
(Phyllis produces several movie magazines.)
After all of my efforts to teach her some sense
And to raise her above the cesspit of her breed
She still has the affront to procure and to read
Movieola and *Photoplay* under my roof!
Don't stand there and gape at me — Look, here's the proof!
HENRY.
What the — !
PHYLLIS.
        Instead of Gabbitt or Steinbeck or Frost,
Writers of art and truth, she would rather get lost
With slang that destroys every bit of our language,
With hot jazz and hoodoo and all of that sewage;
A fantasy world that's deceitful and shallow
Of Gable and Lombard and Hepburn and Harlow!

HENRY.
This is the wrong that you deem unforgivable?
PHYLLIS.
Can you not see she's made life here unlivable?
HENRY.
If you say so.
PHYLLIS.
         I say? So you'd pardon her crime?
HENRY.
Of course not, my darling.
PHYLLIS.
                Just look at this slime!
We live in a time of depression and need
Which I've tried to instruct her on, yet she will feed
On this gossip as people go hungry and cold —
Her conscience is really a thing to behold!
MAGDA.
You don't tell me hunger; I know it with style!
So I go to the pictures — Forget for a while.
PHYLLIS.
You impudent baggage, what gives you the right
To forget people's anguish and laugh through the night?
MAGDA.
When you live like I do, you do not have much choice.
But the movie, he give my small hope a big voice;
I go to Times Square and one nickel I'm spending
And see Fred Astaire give to me happy ending.
PHYLLIS.
There we go — She admits it! She'd rather refuse
All my teaching than put it to its proper use!
SYLVIA.
Happy endings are fictions which cripple the brain.
Can you not understand this? Here, let me explain:
It's your duty to be more acutely aware
Of the world and its troubles, 'cause life isn't fair.
It's only by facing the poor and the strange
With a cold steady eye that we'll ever see change.
MAGDA.
You look from Park Avenue at the poor smugly,
But me, I live there and I tell you, it's ugly.

PHYLLIS.
Oh you may as well talk to a brick; she can't hear!
Are you deaf? You got paprika stuck in your ear?
SYLVIA.
Don't you see, as a girl from the low working class,
You should heed what we say and not simply let pass
Such a gold opportunity; you shouldn't bite
Hands that feed food for thought, Magda. It isn't right.
MAGDA.
I don't bite; she don't let me taste food that I cook!
Is it really so wrong to read small movie book?
SYLVIA.
(To Phyllis.)
I thought girls from Europe would be better bred,
But this one's a dud; from the neck up, she's dead.
MAGDA.
I love movie because for a little each week,
I pretend life is beautiful, happy, and chic.
PHYLLIS.
Oh, my head will explode!
SYLVIA.
                              To believe in these lies
Is obscene when the truth stares you right in the eyes.
MAGDA.
You want ugly truth? You can have it! Not me.
I have lived ugly truth; I want nice things to see.
PHYLLIS.
Throw the witch out! Henry, husband, this is pure hell!
Be a man and expel this depraved Jezebel.
HENRY.
Dearest Magda, I'm sorry, but you cannot stay.
However, for severance, you'll get two weeks' pay.
PHYLLIS.
You're joking of course, Henry — No! Not one dime!
Why should she get a penny for wasting our time?
HENRY.
Very well. As you say, Phyllis. Magda, goodbye.
(Magda bursts into tears.)
There, there. Now don't do that. Please, Magda. Don't cry.
(Magda exits, crying.)
Are you happy now, Phyllis? She's fired, she's canned;

Though I'll tell you this much, I don't understand
Why on earth you'd kick up such a holy ordeal
And dismiss a fine cook who makes art of a meal
Over something as petty as some magazine.
PHYLLIS.
Henry, this is beyond you, so don't intervene.
I work, slave, and toil to maintain my domain
And refuse to put up with the torture and pain
Of ingratitude, apathy, blindness, and scorn
From a meathead like Magda. It cuts like a thorn
In my heart when I think of the efforts I took
To improve that drab nincompoop's social outlook;
And this is the thanks that I get for my trouble!
SYLVIA.
As folks work and struggle with lives turned to rubble
To set their lives straight and put food on their table,
That lummox would rather sit watching Clark Gable!
To have a domestic who lowers the tone
With such heartless dispassion, we cannot condone.
HENRY.
But what does it matter if she likes the pictures
As long as she cooks well? She don't need your strictures
On politics or how there's folks in a crunch —
What the blazes does that have to do with my lunch?
Since when does enjoying the Marx Brothers mean
That she'll not do her job well or serve bad cuisine?
All your talk about soup kitchens, breadlines, and such,
Won't convince me to eat there — So thanks very much!
I would rather a yokel who cooks a good roast
Than a cultured domestic who burns all the toast.
For all that I care, she could cuss like a sailor,
As long as she knew how to make Magda's quail, or
Those yummy croquettes, or her lamb chops or cakes,
Or that Worcestershire sauce that she served with our steaks!
Your Gabbitt and Steinbeck may be smart and slick,
But I know if I ate what they cooked I'd be sick!
PHYLLIS.
While people go jobless, grow weaker and thinner,
You stand there and rant on and on about dinner!
You're being ridiculous, dull, and obtuse,
Throwing tantrums, behaving like some silly goose.

Be a man who takes action, not simply complains.
Shed your trifling shackles and self-obsessed chains
And for once, think of someone besides your own self.
Try to put your desires and your needs on the shelf;
For one's body is garbage compared to one's soul.
You should strive, as I do, to a more noble goal.
HENRY.
Yes, my body is me, and I treat it with care;
And though garbage it may be, it's still mine to wear.
SYLVIA.
One's body is one part, one's brain is the other;
A body that won't use its brain is a bother.
If you wish to be more than just walking garbage
You need to let logic cure your mental blockage.
Developing more of a strong social conscience
And searching for wisdom that has some real substance
Instead of devoting each short fleeting hour
To what you can feel, smell, debauch or devour
Will give your life purpose and hope and design;
You'll speak like a scholar and no longer whine.
HENRY.
I can't take this. That's it. I've been silent too long.
And though you may deem what I say to be wrong,
I simply cannot hold my tongue one more moment.
I know you consider your projects important,
But have you the tiniest shred of an inkling
That people regard you as foolish and piddling?
They laugh and they mock you behind your own backs.
It upsets me to hear their derisive attacks.
PHYLLIS.
Jealous numbskulls have always been fueled by their spite.
HENRY.
Yes, I thought you might say that. I'm sure you're quite right;
But these are our friends that I'm talking about —
And don't give me that look! I'm the one who should pout,
As your crazy behavior has lost us respect
In the eyes of my colleagues and pals. Intellect
Is a fine thing to have, but what gets up my nose
Is the way that you flaunt facts and figures and pose
As some blue-ribbon brain who's surrounded by clods.
I'm sure your intentions are good, but ye gods —

Our dinner guests don't get to eat their meringues
Without sitting through one of your endless harangues,
Or your lectures on politics, science, the arts,
Which are always accompanied by some big charts
That frighten the help and confuse all our guests
Whom you treat as a bunch of dull fat-headed pests
'Til they flee for their lives looking shellshocked and spent
As you sit there and click your tongue in discontent.
Or those writers, those so-called great minds of our age
You parade through our house like a burley-Q stage
With their boring recitals of novels and verse
That are so deadly awful; but what's even worse
Is that you make me pay for their talent and time
With big checks made to "cash." Do you really think I'm
So enormously stupid and rich to allow
Them to bankrupt me just 'cause you say they're highbrow?
For all of your talk about this harsh Depression,
It certainly hasn't made any impression
On how you throw heaps of my money away
On some charlatan hoax whom you term protégé,
You've a husband and daughters, a house, and a staff
And the way you abuse them all would make me laugh
If it wasn't so awful I just want to cry.
Have you no love or int'rest in us, Phyllis? Why?
If I wanted a spouse who cared less how I felt
Than the plight of the poor, I'd have wed Roosevelt!
PHYLLIS.
Oh, what horrible thoughts and how shockingly phrased!
SYLVIA.
You're a small-minded man, Henry. I am amazed
We're related at all. Why, you make me ashamed
To be known as your sister. The way you've defamed
All our efforts and work with such bile and hate —
You make me despair. I can hardly see straight.
I'm disgusted. I can't even look at your face
As I want no reminders we're of the same race!
(Sylvia exits.)
PHYLLIS.
Have you quite finished now? Is there more on the way?
HENRY.
No, I think that's enough. Or at least for today.

Let's not quarrel, my sweet pea; I hate when we fight.
Phyllis, I'll change the subject. Come, smile. All right?
Our Ramona, though she fills my heart with such pride,
Has no interest, I hear, in becoming a bride.
She's a budding philosopher, so I am told.
And I have no objection. She's brighter than gold.
But our dear little Betty is quite widely sought
And I wonder if you —
PHYLLIS.
                     I have given it thought
And I have just the one. I'm willing to bet he
Will be the most perfect of husbands for Betty.
A man of great wit, whose bright star is ascendant,
On his arm, our daughter will look quite resplendent.
This soul, so divine that all hearts wish to nab it,
Belongs to none other than dear Upton Gabbitt;
A capital choice for our daughter to marry —
If she were a fiddle, he'd be Stradivari
And turn her existence to beautiful music;
If she were a poem, he'd render her epic;
I've told him my thoughts and we strongly agree
He'll be perfect for her. You just leave it to me.
And I won't hear a word of objection from you;
My mind is made up and I've thought it quite through.
I'm tired of constantly being opposed.
Our decision is final. The subject is closed.
(Phyllis exits. Rupert looks in.)
RUPERT.
Well, how did it all go? I see Phyllis has left.
Did you handle the matter with nuance and deft?
HENRY.
Yes.
RUPERT.
     And what's the result? Did she give her consent?
Can young Betty start planning the blessed event?
HENRY.
Not quite yet.
RUPERT.
          She refused?
HENRY.
                    No.

RUPERT.
                           Did she hesitate?
HENRY.
Not at all.
RUPERT.
          Then what gives?
HENRY.
                              She's come up with a mate
Of her own for my daughter.
RUPERT.
                              A mate of her own?
HENRY.
Yes, her mind is made up.
RUPERT.
                      And who is this millstone?
HENRY.
Upton Gabbitt.
RUPERT.
               You're kidding!
HENRY.
                              I wish that I were!
'Cause right now my whole life feels like one ugly blur.
RUPERT.
You've accepted her choice?
HENRY.
                            Are you loopy or what?
RUPERT.
Well then, what did you say?
HENRY.
                              It was much wiser not
To put forth a position when she was so firm.
RUPERT.
At least say you planted the seed or the germ
Of the thought of young Dicky —
HENRY.
                                Well, actually, no;
She seemed so intent on her choice, Rupert, so —
RUPERT.
Oh that's excellent, Henry. No, really. Good work!
Why stand up and assert your will when you can shirk
All your duties as father and head of your house?

Are you really a man or are you a mouse?
If I had a wife, I would not be some schnorrer.
HENRY.
If you had a wife, I would eat my fedora!
I'm sorry there, Rupert, but you aren't married
To Phyllis; try matching her will, you'll be buried
Alive if you so much as rankle her temper.
I find it much better to humor and pamper
Her various moods than to kick up a riot.
I can't take the stress; I prefer peace and quiet.
No matter how much she may talk about reason,
If you disagree with her wishes, it's treason.
She'll crush you like nothing so much as a bug
And destroy you quite utterly; or she will shrug
And, for weeks, sit and sigh as she clenches her fist
And not look at you once, like you ceased to exist.
I know she behaves like a black-shirted bully
But I don't know how to defeat her will — Truly!
RUPERT.
Your cowardice, plainly, is what gives her power.
You bleat like a sheep and obey her and cower
In fear of your life, 's'if she'll tear off your legs.
When a husband sits up like a lapdog and begs,
He will get nothing more than the crumbs he deserves.
If you're really a man, you will shore up your nerves.
Or are you prepared to give up your own daughter
And sacrifice her like a lamb to the slaughter?
Will you abdicate and force Betty to take
Some unbearable pill with the charm of a snake?
No, I cannot believe that a brother of mine
Has a thick yellow stripe running straight down his spine!
I'm telling you, Henry, you'd better think twice
Or your balls will forever be trapped in a vice.
I'm sorry I'm being so vulgar and stern,
But it's high time you started to sit up and learn
How to take care of business beneath your own roof,
'Cause right now, as a husband, you're more of a spoof.
HENRY.
You're right, of course, Rupert. And I get your point.
I'm the man of this house. I'm in charge of this joint.
I must screw up my courage —

RUPERT.
                        That's right.
HENRY.
                                    I'm no punk!
Our mother did not raise a coward — That's bunk!
RUPERT.
That-a-boy!
HENRY.
              After all, Betty's my daughter too,
And who pays for this wedding if not you-know-who!
RUPERT.
There you go!
HENRY.
                She can't use me to mop up the floor.
Mister Nice Guy is gone and he's bolted the door!
RUPERT
Aces up!
HENRY.
                        Wait 'til she gets a load of me now.
Her head will be spinning in place — Holy cow!
RUPERT.
Gee, brother, you sound plenty rugged at last!
HENRY.
Rupert, get on the wire. Get Dicky here fast.
RUPERT.
Yes! Right away, captain! *(On the phone.)* Hello, operator?
HENRY.
This King of Baked Beans will defeat that dictator!

End of Act Two

ACT THREE

Afternoon. Phyllis, Ramona and Sylvia. Upton Gabbitt eating canapés.

PHYLLIS.
Take a seat, ladies — Please! We must start our salon.
The master has penned a new verse to feast on.
RAMONA.
I'm burning to hear it!
SYLVIA.
                My ears are a-quiver!
PHYLLIS.
Our own Upton Gabbitt will stand and deliver
A new work that's never been heard yet before us.
RAMONA.
A reason to sing out hosannas in chorus!
SYLVIA.
It's manna from heaven — A gift from the gods!
PHYLLIS.
And composed in my home! I mean, what are the odds?
RAMONA.
I can't wait!
SYLVIA.
     Do please read it!
PHYLLIS.
                   Come, end the suspense!
GABBITT.
I will humbly submit, ladies. But in its defense
I must state categorically, it's a bit rough.
PHYLLIS.
With a genius like yours, it could be off the cuff.
GABBITT.
In which case it might end up "off-collar" as well.
SYLVIA.
Oh the wit! Ain't he droll!

(Betty appears, sees the group, and turns to go.)
PHYLLIS.
                              Betty! Stay for a spell.
BETTY.
I wasn't aware you were having a meeting.
PHYLLIS.
Dear Gabbitt's about to regale us by reading
A marvelous verse of the utmost importance.
BETTY.
Oh Mother, you know I would be but a hindrance;
I don't know a thing about poetry's beauty
And less about things of importance or duty.
PHYLLIS.
No matter. Come join us and listen to Gabbitt
And later on, sweetheart, I'll tell you a secret.
GABBITT.
The art of the poem should give you no qualms;
There is poetry plenty in your humble charms.
BETTY.
You don't say. Well golly, if you choose to fribble
Your time away scribbling —
SYLVIA.
                              Now Betty, don't quibble.
Sit down with us; bask in his masterwork's glow.
RAMONA.
He's better than Frost. He's our own Cicero.
PHYLLIS.
All right, let's begin. We'll have no more delays.
GABBITT.
I must say, my dears, these are swell canapés.
But on to my poetry — What an ordeal
It is to create. I hope my words can reveal
The strong passion I feel for the subject I chose,
Which, as you all know, has me deep in the throes
Of an artistic crisis, the like I've not known;
It cuts through my flesh all the way to the bone,
And envelops me in such a violent pain
That I hope I don't faint, but can somehow maintain
My composure through speaking my poem right now.
RAMONA.
This is so darn exciting!

PHYLLIS.
                    I'm breathless!
SYLVIA.
                              And how!
GABBITT.
I'll begin it at once!
(Gabbitt clears his throat and is about to read —)
SYLVIA.
Oh, the tension is thrilling!
(Gabbitt adopts another pose and is about to read —)
Good poetry has an effect that's spine-chilling!
PHYLLIS.
If we keep interrupting, he can't say a word!
GABBITT.
"Sonnet — "
SYLVIA.
              Betty, be quiet. He needs to be heard.
(Gabbitt recites in a slow lugubrious tone —)
GABBITT.
  "Sonnet to a Forgotten Man, Begging on a Street Corner for a
    Hot Cup of Joe."
  On the night of November the tenth
  You approached me with jobless menace,
  Your ragged claws of empty promise,
  A road less taken, as you seek strength."
SYLVIA.
Oh, what an opening!
RAMONA.
                    What vivid strong phrases!
PHYLLIS.
His talent and flair will exceed all our praises!
RAMONA.
"Ragged claws" is an image I'll not soon forget.
SYLVIA.
"Road less taken," a vision of loss and regret.
PHYLLIS.
"Jobless menace" is much the best way to describe
That sad poor hungry creature and all of his tribe.
SYLVIA.
Upton, please do continue.

GABBITT.
>"On the night of November the tenth
>>You approached me with jobless menace,
>>Your ragged claws of empty promise,
>>A road less taken, as you seek strength."

RAMONA.
"Ragged claws"!
SYLVIA.
"Road less taken"!
PHYLLIS.
"Jobless menace"!
GABBITT.
>"'Brother!' You said, and halted your step,
>>You child of ashes and dust-heaps,
>>You orphan for whom our cold eye weeps,
>>'Spare a dime for some joe and some pep?'"

SYLVIA.
Oh murder! I hope I can calm my poor heart.
RAMONA.
You must give us a chance to admire every part.
PHYLLIS.
I'm quite out of breath, Mister Gabbitt. I'm speechless.
Your wisdom and insight are quite simply peerless.
RAMONA.
>"'Brother!' You said, and halted your step,
>>You child of ashes and dust-heaps."

Those "ashes and dust-heaps" are so wildly intense,
I can practically smell their exotic incense.
PHYLLIS.
>"'Brother!' You said, and halted your step,"

By calling him brother, he sees we're all one —
Mister Gabbitt, your wisdom has me quite undone.
RAMONA.
Yes, that "Brother" — It took away my very breath.
SYLVIA.
The metaphor's perfect. It's symbolic of death.
PHYLLIS.
But the line (please forgive me if I get it wrong),
The line of "you child" is so terribly strong,
For in those two words is contained such vast knowledge —

RAMONA.
The meaning of which will be studied at college.
SYLVIA.
I'm afraid it's all true. You must take it as fact
That this poem of yours will have massive impact
On the future of poetry, and of this land —
PHYLLIS.
And again, for "you child" you deserve a warm hand.
I just can't remember the last time I heard
A verse so accomplished that its every word
Feels emblazoned upon the contours of my brain —
SYLVIA.
And the tone of the piece, it's so now, so urbane.
GABBITT.
(Modestly.)
He he.
RAMONA.
    "Some joe and some pep" has me in its spell.
When I think of those people who stumbled and fell,
Losing all that they had with the stock market crash —
Oh, it kills me to think of their poor lives: All trash.
PHYLLIS.
In a word, my dear Upton, you've written a gem,
A crowning achievement, a verse diadem.
GABBITT.
There is one more stanza, if you'd care to hear it.
RAMONA.
Another?
SYLVIA.
    My goodness!
PHYLLIS.
        Your words have such spirit!
RAMONA.
Remind us once more of the line, "'Brother!' You said."
GABBITT.
   "'Brother!' You said, and halted your step."
PHYLLIS, SYLVIA and RAMONA.
— "And halted your step."
GABBITT.
"You child of ashes and dust-heaps."

PHYLLIS, SYLVIA and RAMONA.
— Those "Dust-heaps"!
GABBITT.
"You orphan for whom our cold eye weeps."
PHYLLIS, SYLVIA and RAMONA.
It weeps! It weeps!
GABBITT.
"'Spare a dime for some joe and some pep?'"
PHYLLIS.
"Some pep!"
SYLVIA and RAMONA.
Ah!
GABBITT.
  "'Oh my dear brother, forgotten by time!'
   Said I as I gave him a rusty old dime
   'You walk, in beauty, like the night.'"
PHYLLIS, RAMONA and SYLVIA.
Ah!
GABBITT.
  "'So strongly stand stiff and stick up for your fight!
   Brother, regardless of what some fools say,
   Tomorrow is another day!'"
PHYLLIS.
It's too much for me, girls!
SYLVIA.
                   I'll faint!
RAMONA.
                           Oh, what bliss!
PHYLLIS.
Have you ever heard anything better than this?
RAMONA.
"So strongly stand stiff and stick up for your fight!"
SYLVIA.
"Brother, regardless of what some fools say — "
PHYLLIS.
    "Tomorrow is another day!"
That's so true, oh so true; oh dear Upton: applause!
RAMONA.
Rich feeling and insight to give us all pause.
SYLVIA.
I am just overwhelmed by its wisdom profound.

PHYLLIS.
I am dumbstruck in awe by such passion unbound.
RAMONA.
It heralds new hope in what is achievable.
GABBITT.
Then you consider it —
PHYLLIS.
                      Quite unbelievable!
No one has tackled the issues as you do.
SYLVIA.
What's wrong with young Betty? She looks like some voodoo
Has taken ahold of her senses. She's glum!
BETTY.
We have different ways and march to our own drum.
A genius for verse doesn't come just by praying.
GABBITT.
My poetry bores you. Is that what you're saying?
BETTY.
No, I paid no attention.
PHYLLIS.
                    Shall we have another?
RAMONA.
Oh Betty, buck up. Can't you be more like Mother?
GABBITT.
"Ode to a Discarded Shoe Found by the Author Outside the Grand Central Station."
PHYLLIS.
His titles are always so rich and inventive.
SYLVIA.
Their novelty makes all his listeners attentive.
GABBITT.
  "Oh, thou lost and soulless loafer — "
SYLVIA, RAMONA and PHYLLIS.
Ah!
GABBITT.
  "Skin like leather; did a chauffeur
    Cast you out of his car window
    On his drive's hasty crescendo?
    Are those holes and broken laces
    Memories of well-trod faces?
    Did your arch support the New Deal

    Or are you, like me, a heel?"
PHYLLIS.
What erudition and wit and such cleverness!
SYLVIA.
I can practically feel that shoe's shabbiness.
GABBITT.
    "Are those holes and broken laces
    Memories of well-trod faces?
    Did your arch support the New Deal
    Or are you, like me, a heel?
    'No,' the shoe said with its tongue tip,
    'I'm no loafer, I'm a wingtip!'"
RAMONA.
"A wingtip" — I didn't expect that. How grand!
PHYLLIS.
No one writes like you do with such polished command.
SYLVIA.
    "'No,' the shoe said with its tongue tip,
    'I'm no loafer, I'm a wingtip!'"
Here the symbol and metaphor both coincide
And infuse the downtrodden with elegant pride.
PHYLLIS.
We are humbled, dear Upton, by your *savoir faire*.
Compared to you, we must seem dowdy and square.
GABBITT.
Not at all, my dear Phyllis. In fact, the reverse;
And what's more, I would love to read some of your verse.
PHYLLIS.
Oh, you flatter me, Upton. You're terribly sweet.
But I've written no poems; it's too mean a feat;
Though I do have a book that I'm laboring on
Which I sometimes recite from here at our salon.
I've penned eighty chapters of this exegesis
On social reform and the future. My thesis
Improves and updates Plato's musty *Republic*
(An incomplete work that's both dull and lethargic).
It seeks to examine through deep exploration
The fate of all womanhood in our fair nation;
For men have too long been in charge of our yearning
And kept us sequestered from knowledge and learning.
They deem us too flighty to have an opinion,

Preferring instead an obedient minion
Who shrinks like a violet, keeps a neat house,
And in all worldly matters stays mum as a mouse.
RAMONA.
It's deeply degrading to be so maligned;
They would have all our cares and concerns be confined
To what hat is in fashion, what dress is the rage,
And what gossip now fills the society page.
SYLVIA.
Men think we are gorgeous but dumb; it's insulting.
But we'll put them wise; we'll fight back. We're revolting!
GABBITT.
My regard for you ladies is known far and wide.
I enjoy nothing more than a gal by my side,
But I always respect them as equals — No less.
PHYLLIS.
That's because you're perceptive and sensitive. Yes,
Together we'll prove that we know how to gauge
And evaluate issues like minimum wage —
SYLVIA.
Or this Social Security nonsense.
PHYLLIS.
                            My dears —
That dumb plan will go bankrupt in less than ten years!
These problems affect everyone, not just men.
Why should we keep all quiet and meek?
SYLVIA.
                                       Well, amen!
With the coming election, we'll leave our boudoir
And go canvass for votes to defeat F.D.R.
PHYLLIS.
The man is a menace.
RAMONA.
                      His wife's the real danger.
SYLVIA.
She looks like she'd be most at home in a manger.
RAMONA.
Those teeth!
PHYLLIS.
          And that face, why I just want to smack it!

SYLVIA.
She could eat an apple through a tennis racket.
GABBITT.
The Socialist Party presents the best hope.
PHYLLIS.
That Republican Landon just hasn't the scope.
RAMONA.
As for me, I'm a Communist, as you all know.
SYLVIA.
People talk about Jefferson, Locke, and Rousseau,
But that Machiavelli sure set a good trend
When he said that the means are subsumed by the end.
GABBITT.
I recently read a fine pamphlet by Lenin.
Though Trotsky, I hear, is more favored by women.
RAMONA.
I do love his speeches.
PHYLLIS.
      But they're so long-winded.
RAMONA.
Perhaps, but there's one thing he's not, and that's timid.
There's lots we can learn from the Soviet model.
GABBITT.
The State should give work to the people, not coddle
Or pamper them endlessly with these New Deals.
SYLVIA.
Trotsky looks like a Jew — Have you seen the newsreels?
PHYLLIS.
Well, at least he's not colored. But ladies, let's shift
Our talk to a topic that caused quite a rift
At our previous meeting; I mean, of course, Spain.
SYLVIA.
Not that again, Phyllis; the subject's a pain.
It is clear as can be Franco should be in charge
Of that mess of a country; I mean, by and large,
People like having leaders who take strong control.
RAMONA.
You mean like Herr Hitler?
SYLVIA.
      Why not? Oh the whole,
He's done a fair bit for his country's finances.

RAMONA.
How can you believe those Teutonic romances?
SYLVIA.
Come on now Ramona, don't nitpick and dicker —
RAMONA.
And who'd want to wear that atrocious swastika?
PHYLLIS.
See, it's clear, Upton, we know our current events
And have as much insight and plain common sense
As our male counterparts who discuss world affairs.
We women deserve to have our equal shares
In policy-making which shapes the world's globe.
It is our firm commitment to seek and to probe
Modes of knowledge to further perpend and discern
Things that stand as examples from which we can learn
And advance our society out of the past
To a future of fairness and wisdom at last.
(The doorbell rings.)
PHYLLIS.
Who on earth could that be?
SYLVIA.
      Was someone expected?
RAMONA.
I'll see the intruder is promptly ejected.
GABBITT.
Forgive me, dear ladies; it's not an intruder.
I hope you don't think me excessively rude or
Unmannered, but I took a chance and invited
A colleague who wanted to meet you.
PHYLLIS.
      Delighted!
(To a servant:)
Show him in there, you — What's-it; it seems we're in luck —
Here's a chance to show off our wit, wisdom, and pluck.
(Betty goes to exit.)
Wait! Betty, I told you I wanted you here.
BETTY.
But for what?
PHYLLIS.
   Patience, darling; all soon shall be clear.
(Ramona has shown in T.S. Bains.)

GABBITT.
Dear ladies, with pleasure I hereby present
A fine gentleman who swears he can't be content
'Til he makes your acquaintance; for you, he maintains,
Are the doyens of culture. My friend, T.S. Bains.
PHYLLIS.
Any friend of yours, Upton, is welcome *chez nous*.
GABBITT.
He's a wonderful writer who scored quite a coup
With his latest novella which Steinbeck adored.
PHYLLIS.
Mister Steinbeck himself? Mister Bains, but I'm floored!
SYLVIA.
You know Steinbeck?
RAMONA.
      Oh, Steinbeck! The man is a god!
PHYLLIS.
What's he like?
SYLVIA.
    Is he tall?
RAMONA.
      Is he kind?
PHYLLIS.
        Is he odd?
SYLVIA.
They say that he drinks.
RAMONA.
      But I'm sure that's a lie.
PHYLLIS.
Oh, come let us embrace you or we'll simply die!
(T.S. Bains embraces and kisses them all except for Betty, who declines.)
BETTY.
I've never read Steinbeck; I'm not a big fan.
PHYLLIS.
Mister Bains is our guest. Do be nice to the man.
BAINS.
I hope you'll forgive this impassioned intrusion
Of what is quite clearly a heady profusion
Of intellect, learning, and high moral fiber.
PHYLLIS.
We're honored to meet a renowned fellow scriber.

GABBITT.
Mister Bains is accomplished in verse and in prose,
And I'm sure if you asked him, he'd read *quelque chose.*
BAINS.
I despise authors who always monopolize
Conversations by reading some work that they prize;
Making everyone wait for their dinner or drinks
As he slowly repeats some dull phrase which he thinks
Is the zenith of talent, the height of all craft,
When in fact it's old-fashioned or hackneyed or daft.
Writers write to be read, not to stand and recite
Every word that they pen, boring people all night
With lugubrious tones and a voice like a mule.
A writer who reads his own work is a fool.
He belongs to that type of insatiable leech
Begging praise at rich houses with eloquent speech
As he soaks up their food and their booze and their cash
Which they give him 'cause they don't know good art from trash.
So you won't catch me reading my work here out loud.
Here's some verses on love of which I'm rather proud.
GABBITT.
Your poetry holds so much beauty and light.
BAINS.
I could sit up and read your own verses all night.
GABBITT.
The verbal economy which you employ!
BAINS.
Your construction's a gem, like an intricate toy.
GABBITT.
I have read your novella, the story's design
Far exceeds anything I have seen — It's divine.
BAINS.
But your poems? I mean, even Faulkner could learn
From your metaphors. Upton, you've talent to burn.
GABBITT.
But nothing's as good as your "Ode to Old Glory."
BAINS.
Your "Tale of Two Dogs" is the best allegory.
GABBITT.
Your rhyme-scheme breaks new ground; your imagery's haunting.

BAINS.
You set a new standard; to reach it is daunting.
GABBITT.
A master like you should be hailed, venerated.
BAINS.
That Eugene O'Neill should be humbled, prostrated.
GABBITT.
You're our next poet laureate, none else will do.
BAINS.
Who needs John Dos Passos with genius like you!
I wonder, could you take a look for a minute
At this little poem —
GABBITT.
                       Do you know the sonnet
About a man begging for help on the street?
BAINS.
Yes, Ayn Rand had a copy of it at her suite.
GABBITT.
Do you know the author?
BAINS.
                          I hear he's a phony;
At least that's what Ayn says; his sonnet's baloney.
GABBITT.
That's funny, for many consider it vivid.
BAINS.
Oh trust me, dear Upton, the thing is insipid.
Ayn read it out loud and we laughed ourselves sick.
GABBITT.
I'm sure that's because she just read it too quick.
A poem like that must be mulled and digested.
BAINS.
If I wrote like that, I'd be promptly arrested.
GABBITT.
And I say one can't write a more perfect sonnet.
I should know, because it is my name that's on it.
BAINS.
You? Hush my mouth, no!
GABBITT.
                    Yes.
BAINS.
                          But Upton, that's horrid!

GABBITT.
You thought it was laughable, shallow, and florid!
BAINS.
Not at all! As you said, she just read it too fast;
Or perhaps my attention had flagged to half-mast.
But enough about this, let's consider my verse.
GABBITT.
I have one thing to say about that: "Hello, nurse!"
It's so weak and old-fashioned, it longs for the grave,
And I've seen sharper wit last time I had a shave.
BAINS.
The imagery works well; Ayn Rand called it charming.
GABBITT.
There's more charm in leaflets about cattle farming.
BAINS.
I'm not bothered by that; diff'rent strokes, diff'rent folks.
GABBITT.
Anyone who'd like your work has had sev'ral strokes.
BAINS.
Just because it's not written for pedants or bores — !
GABBITT.
Don't confuse me with those attributes which are yours.
BAINS.
Abercrombies like you have no clue about art.
GABBITT.
You're a fine one to talk, you uncouth Southern fart.
BAINS.
And to think I admired your work. You're a hack!
GABBITT.
You want a swift left to the jaw for that crack?
BAINS.
Don't kid yourself, Gabbitt, I'd clobber ya silly!
GABBITT.
I mean it — I'll give you a shiner — A dilly!
BAINS.
Ayn was right; you're a joke; a deluded sad fake.
GABBITT.
Put 'em up or get out, Bains, 'cause that takes the cake!
BAINS.
Oh, you talentless cracker —

PHYLLIS.
                        Please! What's this about?
GABBITT.
He's all wet, this imposter — Just look at him pout.
Go jump in the river, you plagiarist sham!
BAINS.
I would if I wrote trash like yours, you big ham!
Your "Tale of Two Dogs" leaves its readers with fleas.
GABBITT.
Yeah, well, your "Ode to Old Glory" just flaps in the breeze.
BAINS.
You're so bad that your publisher slit his own throat.
GABBITT.
That's because he had read that novella you wrote.
BAINS.
Read the critics' response to my work and despair.
GABBITT.
Read what they said about me as well, if you dare.
BAINS.
I am deeply contented with every review
For they prove without doubt I'm superior to you.
Critics may give slight jabs on occasion, but that
Happens to all great writers who step up to bat;
Whereas your work is constantly skewered to bits,
Reducing the critics to venomous fits.
GABBITT.
For that very same reason I hold pride of place.
They lump you with all of the dross. In your case,
One slight jab is enough to dismiss your dull rhyme
Just like all of those hacks who are ten to a dime.
Whereas me, they regard as a singular foe,
Far too strong to be knocked down by one trifling blow.
To them you're unworthy, a punk, secondary,
While I am a noble and strong adversary.
BAINS.
Compared to your bunkum, my poetry shines.
GABBITT.
Feed me alphabet soup, I could crap better lines.
BAINS.
I challenge you, sir, to a match to the death.

GABBITT.
Bring your Remington over and type your last breath.
(T.S. Bains exits, slamming the door after him.)
Please don't blame me for losing my temper with him.
I tried to protect your keen judgment from dim,
Base attacks like he hurled at my sonnet just now.
PHYLLIS.
I'll devote all my strength to resolving this row.
But let us discuss something nice. Come here, Betty.
I've long been concerned that your mind's far too petty
And wrapped up in matters that lack any substance,
But now I've a way to give ease to my conscience.
BETTY.
Please don't trouble yourself, Mother, on my behalf;
I know less about poetry than a giraffe.
I'm content with my life, which is simple and plain,
I have little ambition, and can't stand the strain
Of these heady discussions in which you take part;
I would rather stay stupid than act like I'm smart,
For the effort it takes seems exhausting indeed.
What I know isn't much, but it's all that I need.
PHYLLIS.
Dear daughter, it causes me no end of shame
For a person so simple to share my own name.
All the beauty you have, which is much, is skin-deep:
Like a flower, it fades; but pure wisdom will keep
And enrich your existence in more ways each day
Than a nice pair of legs, which are after all clay.
For that reason I've searched high and low for a scheme
To inspire in your heart all those traits I esteem
And infuse in your mind the importance of wit,
Education, and learning. At last I have hit
On the answer which will make these wishes come true
And that is the joining in marriage of you
With a man who is erudite, cultured, and wise;
I mean, Mister Gabbitt, of course. He's a prize
And a wonderful choice as a husband, my dear.
See, there's hope for you yet, so rejoice in good cheer.
BETTY.
What, me, Mother?

PHYLLIS.
>   Yes. It's high time you grew up.
SYLVIA.
Dear Upton, I'm sorry; don't be a sad pup.
Though your heart aches for me, I surrender its hold;
This union will bring you successes untold.
So go and be happy, although your heart breaks.
GABBITT.
I cannot express, madam, how my soul quakes
With such joy and delight — Why, it can't be surpassed!
BETTY.
You'd better slow down a bit, bub. Not so fast!
I've not said "I do" —
PHYLLIS.
>   What a strange thing to say!
Now Betty, be nice to your new fiancé.
Why isn't she smiling? I don't understand.
GABBITT.
I can hold back no longer. I must kiss your hand.
(Gabbitt kisses Betty's hand. She stares, horrified and mute.)
PHYLLIS.
Ah, she's speechless with joy. She needs time to reflect.
GABBITT.
We'll share in a future you'd never expect.
And though parting's sweet sorrow — Farewell now, my own!
(Phyllis, Gabbitt, and Sylvia exit.)
RAMONA.
The deep love and care that our mother has shown
You is only surpassed by her choice of that man.
BETTY.
Why not take him yourself if you're such a big fan?
RAMONA.
He was granted to you as a groom, not to me.
BETTY.
You're the older one here, so please take him. Feel free.
RAMONA.
If the concept of marriage appealed to me, sis,
I would certainly take him with unequaled bliss.
BETTY.
If my head was like yours and so stuffed full of trash,
Such a union would not seem so stupid or brash.

RAMONA.
Although our thoughts differ on which course of action
Is best, we should not cause a breach or infraction
To our mother's trust, but obey her desire,
Regardless of whether you see it as dire.
(Henry enters, with Uncle Rupert and Dicky.)
HENRY.
Come here, Betty; it's time you approved of my plan
And accepted the hand of this wonderful man
As your husband. No arguments! Do as you're told.
You will thank me one day when you're both good and old.
(Betty rushes to Dicky's side and takes his hand.)
RAMONA.
I see you're inclined to accept Father's notion.
BETTY.
The will of our parents deserves our devotion;
It's best not to cause any breach or infraction.
RAMONA.
Our mother will wish an immediate retraction.
HENRY.
Meaning what?
RAMONA.
            Meaning she will have something to say
On your choice and selection of her fiancé.
She has someone in mind —
HENRY.
                     Shut your trap, saboteur!
If you want to be flapping your gums, go see her;
Don't be sticking your nose where it doesn't belong —
That goes double for her. I've put up for too long
With the bunch of you hags and your silly pretense.
So go tell her my plans, I don't give two red cents
What she thinks or intends. Betty's my daughter too!
So go on then and get!
(Ramona exits quickly.)
RUPERT.
              Brother, I'm proud of you!
DICKY.
Sir, it feels like the whole world's against us. What now?
HENRY.
To be honest, I'm not really sure as to how,

But I'd stake all my beans this'll somehow end well.
(Dicky and Betty kiss and embrace.)
Take a look at that sight, brother. Ain't that just swell?
My heart is well pleased to see Betty so merry;
It makes the whole house feel much brighter and airy
And brings back fond memories of my own youth —
(As they watch Dicky and Betty walk off together, arm in arm.)
We can only stay young doing good, that's the truth.

End of Act Three

ACT FOUR

The cocktail hour. Ramona and Phyllis. Servants preparing drinks.

RAMONA.
Yes! Without any wavering, she acquiesced
And, pretending obedience, grossly transgressed
And received Dicky's hand. Oh, I tried to apprise
Her of what she was doing. But it's no surprise
Betty listens to Father and flaunts your commands.
She was always his darling. I know where she stands!
PHYLLIS.
I see I must clear up a mind deeply cluttered
And teach her which side of her bread has been buttered.
It's time that she learned what obedience means;
And your poor silly father should stick to his beans
And not stick his fat nose in the fine plans I've made.
She will follow my wishes. *(To a servant.)* Not gin; lemonade.
RAMONA.
Dad should have at least tried to ask or consult you
Instead of enforcing his will which insults you;
While Dick should have never ignored your objection.
PHYLLIS.
I'll put a quick end to this so-called connection
Between him and Betty. I don't like his style;
He's known I'm an author for quite a long while,
But not once has he asked me to read him my book!
(Dicky enters, unseen by either lady.)
RAMONA.
The thing to do now is, by hook or by crook,
To make sure those two don't stand a chance to be wed.
And I'll say it upfront, so that no one's misled:
This has nothing to do with my feelings at all.
That Dick jilted and ditched me and still has the gall
To come over and show his fat mug at our house

Doesn't irk me one bit. I don't care. I won't grouse.
But to treat you with such disrespect and contempt —
I mean, Mother, by rights you should foil his attempt
At procuring my sister to have as his bride.
His insolent manner, his rudeness, and snide
Way of doing whatever he wants must be stopped.
At least the good news is, the other shoe dropped
With plenty of time left to do what you have to.
I'm sorry to say this, but he never liked you.
PHYLLIS.
That two-faced baboon!
RAMONA.
      Every time I'd point out
What a genius you are, he would snort, "Yes, no doubt."
PHYLLIS.
Oh, the brute!
RAMONA.
   I once read him that treatise you wrote
And he said it was really no reason to gloat.
PHYLLIS.
Oh, the upstart!
RAMONA.
    We argued for hours on end,
And although he was wrong, he would simply not bend.
DICKY.
(Stepping forward.)
Gee whiz, am I late for my own crucifixion?
Or is this a lecture on how to write fiction?
RAMONA.
How dare you sneak up and eavesdrop?
PHYLLIS.
       Oh, the savage!

DICKY.
Look, would you please tell me without taking umbrage
What harm have I done? Am I wolf in sheep's clothing?
What action of mine rates such eloquent loathing?
Do you want to destroy me and drown all my hope?
Maybe Betty was right when she said, let's elope,
But I nixed that idea 'cause my love is no shame.
So why do you seek to heap censure and blame
With such spite and aversion? Come tell me — what gives?

And what's it to you how the other half lives?
RAMONA.
If indeed I were angry as you seem to think,
I could give ample proof what a fake and a fink
You have been; you deserve every name in the book
For the way that you promised and pledged, then forsook
Vows of love and fidelity; what kind of gent
Swears eternal devotion when it's never meant?
It were better that you should go hungry and poor
Than to gain by my loss. Faithless hearts are impure.
DICKY.
You'd call my heart faithless when it was your pride
Which forced it to find that which yours can't provide?
RAMONA.
Me?
DICKY.
    I played by your rules — You kept changing the game;
If this gets up your nose, search yourself for the blame.
RAMONA.
How dare you!
DICKY.
              Two years I spent dreaming that somehow
I'd meet your steep standards, but I wasn't highbrow
Enough for your liking; my loving attention
Was met with disdain and abrupt condescension.
A dog would be treated with more approbation!
To think I put up with your crass degradation
Without a complaint.
RAMONA.
              Ha!
DICKY.
                    What, you don't understand?
Look, instead of your fist, I reached out for a hand
That was open to mine and which valued my heart.
And Ramona, consider: You played a large part
In the way things turned out here. I'm sorry you're miffed,
But the fault is your own. I'm the one who got stiffed.
RAMONA.
You would call it my fault that I tried to instill
In you some sense of honor and cast off the swill
Of degenerate lust which you wrongly term "love"?

That word connotes wisdom: A gentle kid glove,
Not the groping and fumbling of physical heat
Like two animals rutting, or pawing raw meat.
If I gave you the brush, it was only to teach
You that love is best felt when it's just out of reach.
Can you not overcome your repulsive desire
For sex and carnality? Is there no higher,
More lofty expression to your admiration
Than trying to lure me to lewd fornication?
What good is a union that's based in one's body
Compared to a marriage of minds?
PHYLLIS.
        Pretty shoddy.

RAMONA.
A principled, moral, and ethical soul
Doesn't bother himself with the low sordid role
Of the physical being we're forced to endure;
If you don't know that, you're a, what —
PHYLLIS.
        Epicure.

RAMONA.
Sex is just a distraction, a runaway train;
Love loves for love's sake, not for what it can gain.
DICKY.
That's all very nice and poetic; but seeing
As I'm just a worthless and low human being,
I was born with a body as well as a soul,
And though no Adonis, I'm also no troll,
And I don't think it fair to consign it to dust
Just because it might lead one to passion or lust.
Mind and body together must function as one;
For if only one's soul's in control, where's the fun?
And why should one's body be cast from the picture?
There's much to be learned from its swell architecture.
You're right to believe in the pure, wise, and noble,
But people like me aren't clever or able
To grasp such high concepts; it's far too refined
For my work-a-day brain and my narrow young mind.
You've said (and again, you're quite right) that I'm coarse.
I read no great books, help the poor, or endorse
Any special political views of my own,

But love is, to me, like a mighty cyclone
Which wraps mind and body together in bliss.
Tell me, what kind of feeling is greater than this?
To adore a whole person, their thoughts and their looks,
Is a joy that's far richer than those found in books.
And to flatly condemn it seems frankly quite sad
When its pleasures, I'd hoped, would instead make you glad.
RAMONA.
Do you mean it? Well gee — Since you put it like that,
And insist on your feelings and all of that tat,
And refuse to take council from all that I've said,
There's not much I can do, as you're not better bred;
But if Mother permits me, I'm willing to try
To consent to your wishes. Will that satisfy?
DICKY.
I'm sorry, Ramona, you're simply too late.
I'm in love with another and I'd really hate
To dismiss or refuse, or in any way hurt
My beloved because now you're choosing to flirt.
PHYLLIS.
Mister Mayhew, consider: You need my consent
If to marry my Betty is still your intent.
And has it occurred to you, I might already
Have someone in mind as a husband for Betty?
DICKY.
Mrs. Crystal, I beg you to draw off that choice!
I know I'm not rich; I don't own a Rolls Royce;
In fact, I could barely afford when I cabbed it
To get here tonight, but to lose to that Gabbitt
Seemed such a disgraceful and horrible fate,
I would willingly pay any overpriced rate
Just to stop such a wrong-headed match; he's a dolt!
If you force him on Betty, she's sure to revolt.
I mean, for pete's sake, she can't stomach that sap
With his laughable poems — He gives a bum rap
To those writers who try to create something real
And who honestly try to achieve an ideal.
But he doesn't fool anyone, they see right through
His pretensions and nonsense. Great guns, why can't you?
You've so much more sense than to fall for those pretzels
He passes for art; and those claims that he wrestles

With forces both deep and profound — What a razz;
There's monkeys in zoos with more brains than he has!
And then there's his looks, take his face — What a corker;
That mug is lampooned in the current *New Yorker*!
But more than just ugly, he's strange — Yes, by far;
Even Harper himself thinks the man's too bizarre.
So I hope you'll forgive me for being this blunt,
But the man is a menace, a mealy-mouthed runt.
PHYLLIS.
It's hardly surprising to hear such aspersions
From someone whose mind is so packed with perversions.
(Enter Gabbitt.)
GABBITT.
Holy smoke! I just had the most wonderful dream.
Because of the brilliance of our smart little team
Of progressive political thinkers and minds,
I was flown off to Sweden where they hailed my lines
Of poetical verse as beyond parallel,
And they gave me that peace prize from Mister Nobel.
PHYLLIS.
I am certain your dream will some day be a fact,
But let's talk of it later. This man has attacked
All our values; it's clear wisdom's wasted on him.
He considers political thought rather dim.
DICKY.
It seems that some clarification's in order.
To say I find politics dim's to embroider
The truth; what I mean is, I hate when it's used
As a fist against all who are poor and abused
By the rich and conceited who think they know best.
So-called "wisdom" like that only gets me depressed.
GABBITT.
There will always be people who know more than some;
It's the role of the wisest to govern the dumb.
DICKY.
To say that they're wise just because they have money
Is downright ridiculous; Gabbitt, you're funny.
GABBITT.
I'm saying that learning can give men the tools —
DICKY.
The greater that learning, the greater the fools.

GABBITT.
That's a strange paradox.
DICKY.
                       Hey, without any strain,
I could show you some proof of how dense and inane
Those with learning can be. To give an example,
I won't have to go far. The proof here is ample.
GABBITT.
I don't see any proof here which you could compose.
DICKY.
The proof is as plain as the tip of my nose.
GABBITT.
I always thought ignorance was the prime cause
Of foolish behavior or bad sets of laws.
DICKY.
An ignorant man lacking all education
Ain't as bad as a fool who feigns cultivation.
GABBITT.
Your logic is faulty, your argument's lame.
An uncultured man is a fool — They're the same.
DICKY.
They can't be more different, I do not concur;
A fool is much more like a pompous poseur.
GABBITT.
The first term implies an innate lack of wit.
DICKY.
It's knowledge that makes of the second a twit.
GABBITT.
You're wrong, kid, for knowledge is its own requital.
DICKY.
I can't stand how knowledge makes fools feel entitled.
GABBITT.
You're mighty obsessed with the ignorant rabble
To try to defend them with all of this babble.
DICKY.
It's fools who obsess me; those hypocrite schnooks
Who pack drivel and lies into all of their books.
GABBITT.
Those writers you mention may have higher aims
Than some folks I see here. I'm naming no names.

DICKY.
What you say could be true, but of course, that's a leap;
Some folks don't set much store by such talk. Talk is cheap.
PHYLLIS.
Mister Mayhew, now really — !
DICKY.
                                     You come to his aid?
I'm sure Mister Gabbitt is hardly afraid
Of fighting his battles without your assistance.
RAMONA.
But why do you show such dislike and resistance —
DICKY.
What, you as well, Ramona? Well, heck, I resign.
RAMONA.
Wait — !
PHYLLIS.
        Discussion is welcome, but don't cross the line
By having a laugh at dear Upton's expense.
DICKY.
I've not said a thing that should give him offense.
Besides, he's been mocked by far better than me,
And to all of his critics he's deaf as can be.
GABBITT.
It is hardly surprising to hear such lowbrowed
Opinions from him, when the popular crowd
Is his sole source of reference. Their only concern
Is what's simple and easy; they all hate to learn
Anything that might challenge their tiny brain pan,
Or their ignorant state, of which he is a fan.
DICKY.
Gee, you've so much dislike for the poor working stiff,
Which is really surprising. Your poems all riff
On the plight of those who are facing starvation,
But here you condemn them for their situation,
Proclaiming them fools and calling them shallow.
Do you not consider this attitude callow?
You look down your nose at them, saying they spoil
Our nation's whole future; it makes my blood boil
To hear such hypocrisy and such pretension
From someone who profits from their very mention.
If you could climb down from your big pink balloon

And look at them squarely one bright afternoon,
And open your eyes, you might just recognize
They're not stupid at all; in fact, they're very wise,
'Cause to get through one day in this terrible time
And provide for your kids on, what, less than a dime,
Requires some savvy and skill, which I doubt
You could muster yourself in spite of all your clout.
And because one is poor doesn't mean that one lacks
The good breeding or manners of all of you hacks.
GABBITT.
And where'd you learn manners? Eh, kid? In Hoboken?
DICKY.
Good breeding requires the truth to be spoken.
(The doorbell rings. Ramona exits to answer it.)
So go on and talk art till you're blue in the face,
And explain how your politics really are ace;
Blow your horn about values and morals and life,
How your quaint little poems are chock full and rife
Of intent to improve the forgotten man's fate
As you sit on Park Avenue, loading your plate
With a sycophant's grace and a freeloader's smile,
Pouring on that thick sauce of contempt, scorn, and bile;
For so long as you've someone to pay all your bills,
Why should you give a damn for society's ills?
(Ramona reenters with a letter.)
PHYLLIS.
Ramona, who was that?
RAMONA.
                    A man with a note
From your friend, T.S. Bains.
GABBITT.
                    That insuff'rable goat.
PHYLLIS.
Give it here. Let me see what it says.
RAMONA.
                                This is odd.
It says, "Urgent" and "Open at once." —
(Ramona hands Phyllis the letter. She opens it. Reads.)
PHYLLIS.
                                Oh my God.

(Reading.)

"My dear Mrs. Crystal, greetings and blah blah blah — Hoping that you blah blah — Your precious Gabbitt has been putting out smoke-signals and bragging to anyone who'd listen that he's just about snagged your daughter Betty's hand in marriage. Wingding and what a clambake that would be, if only it weren't for the fact that it's really your money he's after. That's right, your sawbucks, your green stuff, your nice foldin' cabbage. So if I were you, and you were half the woman I take you for, I'd hold off throwing any rice 'til you've read the little poem I've written about him in next week's *Saturday Evening Post*. Until that's published, have a look-see at the enclosed letter, personally written by Mister John Steinbeck on his personal stationary, to attest personally to the shallowness of Mister Gabbitt's person. Yours with humblest blah blah blah — T.S. Bains."
(She looks at the second page.)
"Dear Madam: Upton Gabbitt's parents didn't have any children that lived. Yours, John Steinbeck."
Well, how do you like them green apples, Ramona?
It seems that because of my plans I'm persona
Non grata. No sooner do I plan a marriage,
Then out of their caves they come out to disparage
My virtuous efforts with cavil and quibble.
Well, here's what I think of this scurrilous scribble —
(She tears up the letters and throws the pieces in the air.)
If this little outburst is meant to frustrate me,
Then Bains doesn't know me too well. Just you wait — He
Will see I'm not bullied by his nasty letters.
In fact, they have served to undo what small fetters
Have kept me in check; my resolve has been bolstered.
The next time he comes here, he'd best bring a toaster,
'Cause Betty is marrying Upton tonight.
All this envy and scorn only proves that I'm right.
Ramona, you go fetch us Judge Arbogast,
Then go tell your sister that Dick's been outclassed.
RAMONA.
There's really no point in my talking to Betty,
Your friend here can do that; I'm willing to bet he
Can do more than I to explain your fine verdict
Which makes her feel not like your child, but your convict.
PHYLLIS.
You talk to her, Upton, and if she gets snooty,
Remind her that she must not question her duty.

(Phyllis and Gabbitt exit separately.)
RAMONA.
I'm really not sure how to say that I'm sorry.
I wish I could somehow make things hunky-dory.
DICKY.
I thank you, Ramona; but please don't feel badly.
I won't let him marry her. I love her madly.
RAMONA.
I fear that, regardless, you may not prevail.
DICKY.
I hope I can trust you. You won't tattletale?
RAMONA.
I swear, mum's the word.
DICKY.
                        No, not mum. Try another.
I don't seem to have much good luck with your mother.
RAMONA.
That's all been my fault — Shoulda had better sense.
I hope I can show you some fair recompense.
I'll do what I can to make Betty your bride.
DICKY.
At least I've a chance now with you on my side.
(Ramona exits, as Henry, Uncle Rupert, and Betty enter.)
Sir, without your support, my whole future looks bleak;
I appealed to your wife using every technique
I could think of, but she says that Gabbitt's the man.
HENRY.
Is she nuts? That cold fish? And she calls this a plan?
RUPERT.
Not to worry, with time Phyllis will see the light.
DICKY.
But she plans Betty's marriage to happen tonight.
HENRY.
Tonight?
DICKY.
     That's her plan.
RUPERT.
                    Henry, we'd better hurry
And marry these two.
HENRY.
                 Come now, Betty, don't worry.

DICKY.
But she's sent for the judge who'll perform all the rites.
HENRY.
He'll perform what I want or I'll punch out his lights.
I'm the *pater familias,* lord of my home,
And I tell you my daughter won't marry that gnome.
You come with me, Rupert.
RUPERT.
                            There's much to be done.
HENRY.
And Dick, you come too; you'll quite soon be my son.
(Henry exits.)
BETTY.
I hope that my father will stick to his purpose.
RUPERT.
(Exiting.)
He will. If he doesn't, I'll cause such a ruckus.
DICKY.
Regardless of all of your father's stern bluster,
I feel like I'm living the last stand of Custer.
BETTY.
Oh, Dick, you're my angel; I'm yours till forever.
DICKY.
With you at my side, I can pull through whatever.
BETTY.
I'm scared that my mother may get her own way.
DICKY.
She won't; not as long as I live, anyway.
Come on, who's my baby? Don't worry. Have courage.
BETTY.
I hope that my dad's got the strength to discourage
This hideous plan. If he can't, I'll just die.
I would sooner take poison than marry that guy!
DICKY.
Don't talk like that, Betty. If push comes to shove,
You must never act crazy in proving your love.
(They kiss and Dicky exits.)

End of Act Four

ACT FIVE

After dinner. Betty and Gabbitt.

BETTY.
Mister, look, it's this marriage my mother has planned.
I don't think it's just me; it's got all out of hand.
And I figured, considering all of the mess
And confusion and havoc — I don't have a dress —
And the way that it's tearing this household apart,
And my father's raw nerves — Oh, please don't let me start —
Well, I thought you and I might sit down like adults
To discuss this with logic, and hope what results
Is a friendly solution to this whole affair.
Now I know that you think that in me you will snare
A fine, prosperous, affluent, moneyed young bride.
But to someone who has a philosopher's pride,
And the talent of Steinbeck, why, money's the bunk!
It's a worthless allurement; it's cheap, crass — It's junk!
I know you agree, so for my satisfaction,
Stand by that belief: Put those words into action.
GABBITT.
And I do, for it's not in that way that I'm charmed.
It's your beauty: Your lips, nose, the way your alarmed
Tiny eyes dart in panic around in your head;
It's those things that enchant me; cold water and bread
Would be all that I'd need if I had you as mine.
BETTY.
What a sentiment, sir; what a sweet valentine.
But I'm sorry to say I don't feel that for you.
I respect you of course, but the fly in the goo
Is the fact that I'm already deeply in love.
GABBITT.
With that rude little Dicky?
BETTY.
                Well heaven's above,

It's not something that I can divine or control.
Compared to you, sir, he's an unworthy soul.
Gosh, by any account I'm a fool to prefer
A young lunkhead like Dick. See, I'm no connoisseur.
GABBITT.
The state of our union to which I aspire
Will free you from him and that murky dark mire
Of uninformed thinking. My constant attention
Will wake in your heart my love's fullest dimension.
BETTY.
I don't think so, mister. My heart is too stubborn.
It has its own mind, I fear; nothing can summon
It back from its course. Once its gone, it is gone.
There is simply no hope for that kind liaison
Which you offer. I'm telling you this with respect;
Logic's absent when our hearts decide to select
Whom to favor with love, passion, yearning, and zeal.
It is impulse and whim that decide how we feel.
And I'm sure one could study those whims for a year,
Without learning the reason why someone is dear
While another, who's worthy, just leaves one all cold.
We love whom we love, and that can't be controlled
By advice or by merit; so let me be free,
'Cause there's just no real future between you and me.
GABBITT.
How can I submit to this futile request?
It amounts to my tearing my heart from my breast.
It's impossible, dearest, to fathom the day
When I'd fall out of love with the quaint little way
Which you tease me by keeping me at an arm's length —
BETTY.
Okay, cut the bushwa — I haven't the strength —
Look, I'm sure there are far better fish in the sea.
There are girls who have fortunes far greater than me.
And heck, with that moustache, you'd make such a catch.
GABBITT.
I don't want them, Betty. Can't you see we're a match?
I love you as Abelard loved Eloise;
Like Dante loved Beatrice; like birds love the bees.
BETTY.
I'm serious. Now stop with this silly behavior.

GABBITT.
But can't you see, chipmunk, that you're my heart's savior?
There's not a darn thing that could halt my devotion
To you. Not a word, not an act, spell, or potion.
The bliss that I feel at our coming together
Is worth any pangs of distress you might weather.
Your mother has blessed me and that's worth the struggle
To have you and hold you, to kiss you and snuggle.
BETTY.
But don't you consider it wrong to endorse
This method of making me yours by sheer force?
To marry a girl when she isn't that keen
Can make her behave, on the whole, rather mean;
No matter your ardor and all your browbeating,
She'll find ways to hurt you by lying and cheating.
GABBITT.
I'm not really bothered; those things that you mention
Are easily dealt with. There won't be much tension
As wisdom has cured me of worry and malice,
And logic assures me that, though on the surface,
Your life may seem wretched and boring as hell,
But yet underneath, all will work out just swell.
BETTY.
Gee whiz, mister — That's what I call a good sport!
And to think that philosophy once made me snort.
I'm really impressed! But this fortitude oughta
Be used on a gal from some filthy backwater,
'Cause I wasn't raised to be some blowzy floozy.
The thought of this marriage with you makes me woozy.
So with your permission, I beg you to sever
All thought of this horrible union forever.
GABBITT.
It's no good objecting; you will be my wife.
I have worked far too hard to secure a good life.
So if I were you, I would just grin and bear it.
Now how 'bout a kiss?
BETTY.
                    Sir, I'd first kiss a ferret.
GABBITT.
We'll save it for later. He laughs who laughs last.
I'll be back in a moment with Judge Arbogast.

(Gabbitt exits. Betty grabs up a small statuette and is about to throw it after him, when Henry enters, followed by Dicky and Magda.)
HENRY.
Daughter, come — What's the matter? It's high time we taught
Your mother a lesson. Come and see who I've brought
To help put an end to your mom's domination —
It's Magda; I've had her restored to her station.
BETTY.
(Embracing Magda.)
Oh, Magda, I've missed you — I'm so glad you're back!
I'm very impressed, Dad; now make sure your attack
Doesn't waver or falter when faced with Mom's rage.
It's of vital importance the battle we wage
Shows no weakness. You really must be resolute.
Your word must be final; your will absolute.
HENRY.
Of course! What, you think I'm some kind of pushover?
BETTY.
No, sir.
HENRY.
     Or a fool who obeys and bends over?
BETTY.
Not at all.
HENRY.
      Or perhaps you don't think I can stand
By my word; I'm a coward? A weakling? That's grand!
DICKY.
You're none of those things.
HENRY.
          I will show you the proof
I'm in charge of what goes on here under my roof!
MAGDA.
We know that you will.
HENRY.
        Don't dispute my persistence.
Your mother will learn to obey my insistence.
BETTY.
That's wonderful.
HENRY.
     Ha! You all think it's a crock;
I can tell from the way that you razz me and mock.

DICKY.
If we've made you upset, that was not our intent.
HENRY.
I'm the one who's in charge here — It's me pays the rent!
MAGDA.
You are perfectly right.
HENRY.
     I'm the king of this joint.
DICKY.
That you are.
HENRY.
    My word matters; my will; my viewpoint.
BETTY.
But of course.
HENRY.
     I decide whom my daughter should wed.
DICKY.
Absolutely!
HENRY.
   My power should fill all with dread!
MAGDA.
It does.
BETTY.
  We don't doubt it at all.
HENRY.
      I'm your father,
And what I say goes, 'cause I outrank your mother.
BETTY.
Your word's my command.
DICKY.
      We will follow your bidding.
MAGDA.
We're counting on you, Mister Crystal.
BETTY.
       No kidding!
HENRY.
We'll soon see if Phyllis will dare to oppose
My intentions —
DICKY.
    Remember, it's me that you chose.

BETTY.
They're coming!
HENRY.
            Oh what will I say?
MAGDA.
                        Do not panic.
I help you. Remember: Your wife is satanic.
(Phyllis enters with Judge Arbogast, followed by Sylvia, Ramona, and Gabbitt.)
PHYLLIS.
But Judge, this whole contract is simply pathetic!
Can you not use language a bit more poetic?
JUDGE.
The language is standard and perfectly lawful;
To change even one single word would be awful.
SYLVIA.
Oh, the legal profession just beggars belief —
With their motions, subpoenas, and big dirty briefs.
Where's the art? Where's the culture? Get into your mind
The fact that this household's a bit more refined.
At least write the contract in Latin or French!
JUDGE.
Who, me? If I did, I'd be laughed off the bench.
A contract of marriage is no syllogism.
PHYLLIS.
There's no point in fighting this crass barbarism;
Culture's wasted on him. Judge, don't hover, now sit!
(Seeing Magda.)
Good grief, why's that birdbrain here? Get rid of it!
SYLVIA.
Henry, how could you let in that ungrateful louse?
HENRY.
I can welcome whoever I want to my house.
Now about this whole marriage — And don't look so snide.
JUDGE.
Can we get down to business here? Which one's the bride?
PHYLLIS.
That's her over there. She's my youngest.
JUDGE.
(Greeting Betty.)
                          How do.

HENRY.
This is her special day. We're so proud of —
JUDGE.
(Sneezing.)
                              Achoo!
Pardon me. And the groom?
PHYLLIS.
                    He's that gentleman there.
The smart looking one with the mustache.
HENRY.
                              My heir
And the groom is this gentleman here.
JUDGE.
                         What, two grooms?
I believe that the custom is one.
PHYLLIS.
                    He presumes
That we care for his choice. Write down Upton Gabbitt.
HENRY.
Write down Dicky Mayhew or I will not have it!
JUDGE.
Look here, which one is it? Can you two concur
And pick which one bridegroom you've chosen for her?
PHYLLIS.
Ignore him, Your Honor.
HENRY.
                    Write down what I told you.
PHYLLIS.
Don't listen to him, Judge.
HENRY.
                    Just write Dicky Mayhew.
JUDGE.
Please don't do this to me. I am not a well man.
PHYLLIS.
You heard my instructions!
SYLVIA.
                    Yes, follow the plan!
HENRY.
I will not let my daughter be used as a means
To acquire the fortune I built selling beans.

PHYLLIS.
Oh, I knew you'd embarrass me, Henry. I swear!
He does not want your beans or your money — So there!
HENRY.
Well, Dick is the man that will marry my daughter.
PHYLLIS.
Says you and which army? I won't budge a quarter,
For Upton's my choice. This discussion is over.
JUDGE.
Please make up your minds, in the name of Jehovah!
MAGDA.
This not for a wife to decide. I think father
Should make big decision and say what he'd rather.
PHYLLIS.
Oh brother!
MAGDA.
    A lady should be more polite
And look to her husband to know what is right.
HENRY.
You tell her!
MAGDA.
    Wife in movie does not know her place,
Jimmy Cagney, he put a grapefruit in her face.
PHYLLIS.
Just you try it!
MAGDA.
    If I had a husband, I say,
I treat him like king of the world every day.
But who want man who is soft or compliant?
For me, I take man who is strong like a giant.
And if I cause trouble or make him too cross,
He give me a spanking to show who is boss.
HENRY.
Which is how things should be.
MAGDA.
        Mister Crystal is fair
To want a good man as his son and his heir.
HENRY.
Right.
MAGDA.
  So why you reject Mister Dicky? He's nice

And good-looking and young and polite and he's twice
The man your Mister Upton could be. What would she
Want with ugly and rude husband? Tell this to me.
Okay, so he smart and he speak the good English,
So marry a book! Mrs. Crystal, this foolish.
HENRY.
You have to admit that she's right.
PHYLLIS.
                      Are you done?
MAGDA.
Little *édesem* Betty, she want to have fun.
Gabbitt claim that he care for the poor and the like,
But that is to woman like fish with a bike.
What use social conscience in husband or spouse?
A wife want champagne, caviar, porterhouse,
Not old bread and cold soup. The life of a peasant
May be very noble, but not very pleasant.
I know this; I lived it; and even discussion
Of it will make Betty look like sad old Russian.
If he want to save all the beggars and tramps,
"Good luck," I say, "Go, eat and sleep at their camps
In the Bowery; or, better yet, get a job
And prove you're a mensch, not an arrogant snob."
The proof of men's hearts lies in what they will do,
Not in what they can say.
HENRY.
(To Phyllis.)
                    There we go. Nuts to you!
PHYLLIS.
I've had all I'm willing to stomach. Enough
Of your dimestore philosophy, nonsense, and guff.
And before you attempt to say one more damn word,
I will put down my foot and insist to be heard.
My wish is that Betty will follow my choice
And wed Mister Gabbitt — Keep still! Do not voice
Any word of objection. Don't hem and don't haw.
You've all had your say and my patience is raw.
This marriage will happen, and happen right now;
And if you're distressed 'cause your word or your vow
Was given to Dicky — Well, don't be a moaner;
We do have two daughters, so give him Ramona.

HENRY.
That certainly does sound like one resolution.
Two weddings in one all done by substitution.
BETTY.
Oh, Father!
DICKY.
      Don't do this, I beg you!
SYLVIA.
                        We could
Propose Dick a wife who would make him feel good,
But we'd rather create a more high-minded match
(Although we all know who he'd much rather catch);
This union will teach him a life fair and just,
Without all the nuisance of passion and lust.
(Uncle Rupert enters with papers.)
RUPERT.
Forgive me, I'm sorry to barge in so rudely,
But this couldn't wait so I had to intrude. See,
Two letters arrived with some troubling news.
SYLVIA.
Why, what's wrong, Rupert?
RUPERT.
                    Here. You had better peruse
Them at once. This one's from your attorney, Sam Deans;
This one's from your accountant at Crystal's Canned Beans.
PHYLLIS.
What possible news could Sam Deans have to say
That requires attention on this solemn day?
RUPERT.
Please read it yourself, Phyllis. I can't explain;
I'm too deeply disturbed by the news they contain.
(Rupert hands Phyllis one of the letters. She opens it and reads.)
PHYLLIS.
(Reading.)
"My dear Mrs. Crystal, I have entrusted the delivery of this letter to your brother-in-law Rupert in the hopes that — " blah blah blah get to the point get to the point … "Sad news! I am deeply aggrieved to have to inform you that, because of your negligence in not supplying my clerk with the necessary paperwork, the lawsuit for libel and slander which you have undertaken in the name of Mister Upton Gabbitt against the author T.S. Bains has not been successful."

HENRY.
Lost a lawsuit?!
PHYLLIS.
                    Oh, don't you pretend that you care!
I fight every day for what's decent and fair,
And a setback like this, though distressing and sad,
Won't dissuade me from fighting that arrogant cad.
(Reading.)
"Additionally, I must inform you that, in retaliation, Mr. Bains has entered a countersuit — " Oh jolly! " — which has, sadly, proven successful. As a result of the court's judgment, you are hereby ordered to pay him the sum of forty thousand dollars in damages."
"Ordered"! Who in the blazes does he think he is
To say this to me?
RUPERT.
                    That takes nerve now — Gee whiz!
You're certainly right to feel hurt, scorned, and slighted,
And ought to demand that this rudeness is righted.
He should not have ordered, but begged or requested
You pay forty thousand. You're right to protest it.
SYLVIA.
What's your letter say, Henry?
HENRY.
(Reading.)
"To Mister Henry Crystal, Chairman of the Board, Crystal Canned Beans, Incorporated. Dear sir, I hereby inform you that, due to rising costs in production, and the steady decline in sales over the last fiscal quarter, Crystal Canned Beans is no longer able to offset its debts. Therefore, it is my duty to inform you that you face immediate and irrevocable bankruptcy. Yours, sincerely, Hank Blodget, Accountant for CCB, Inc."
Holy Moses, I'm bankrupt! I'm not worth a fig!
PHYLLIS.
Must you be so emotional? Don't blow your wig!
It's just money. What's money? It's filthy. It's trash.
SYLVIA.
The philosopher's mind doesn't care about cash.
Money's loss is a blessing — it clears the debris
Which clouds reason and truth.
PHYLLIS.
                        Henry, you've been set free!

We can all live quite well on what Upton has saved.
GABBITT.
Just a minute.
SYLVIA.
     What's wrong?
GABBITT.
          Well, the way I've behaved
Has been rude and unthinking: To push for this suit
When it's clear that your daughter does not give a hoot
Or a care for the thought of becoming my bride —
Well, it's wrong.
SYLVIA.
     I'm surprised by the change in your tide!
PHYLLIS.
It strikes me as strange that you choose to revoke
Your kind offer of marriage now that we're quite broke.
GABBITT.
The fact is, I'm tired of their opposition;
Loveless marriage is such a sad proposition.
I could never force Betty into such a state.
PHYLLIS.
And to think I stood by you and thought you were great!
Oh the calumny! Judas! The filthy disgrace!
GABBITT.
You can think what you like of me: Noble or base,
I don't care! Young Betty has broken my heart
So I flatly refuse to stand by and take part
In a marriage which promises me only shame.
Do you know how this union would blacken my name?
I have never been treated so rudely before!
If you people wer'n't broke, I would sue you for sure!
(Gabbitt heads for the door. Henry produces Gabbitt's hat and coat.)
HENRY.
Oh allow me please, sir: Here's your coat and your hat —
(Henry helps him on with his coat. Henry drops the hat. Gabbitt bends over to retrieve it and Henry kicks him out the door.)
Now get out of my house, you cheap freeloading rat!
(Henry slams the door shut.)
PHYLLIS.
Oh Henry, I'm speechless —

RAMONA.
              What a covetous pest!
PHYLLIS.
All he cared for was money! I mean, who'd have guessed?
SYLVIA.
He tried to seduce me, but I just wouldn't budge.
JUDGE.
A fine lady like you deserves better.
SYLVIA.
                    Oh Judge!
DICKY.
Although no philosopher and not a writer,
I can, Mrs. Crystal, attempt to make lighter
The difficult burden your news has inflicted.
You're welcome to move in with me if evicted,
And I will do everything in my small power
To make your life easy in this your dark hour.
PHYLLIS.
Now that is true poetry, Dick. You're a dear.
And to show you my thanks, I will say now and here
That you have my consent, if you're still so inclined —
BETTY.
Not so fast, Mother; no. I have now changed my mind.
I'm sorry, Dick, but I can't marry you now.
DICKY.
What? Betty? What happened? Have I hurt you somehow?
Once your mother agreed, I thought we could be sure —
BETTY.
Oh, but Dick, don't you see? Why, you're terribly poor
And to take on my family — Well, it's not right.
More than anything I wished our marriage just might
Bring an end to your hardship, making life sunny.
But how can we do that without any money?
I love you too much and I cherish your dreams
To inflict on your life such demanding extremes.
DICKY.
With you at my side I can face any trouble;
Without you the whole ball of wax is just rubble.
BETTY.
A passionate love always speaks in this way;
But I fear that the pain of regrets will hold sway

If we try to ignore all the cold and hard facts.
Nothing tears up a marriage or sorely impacts
More than life's small necessities. Husband and wife
Come to hate and resentment when troubles are rife.
RUPERT.
Although all you say is quite true and quite tricky,
Is that the sole reason you won't marry Dicky?
BETTY.
Aside from those worries, my heart is ecstatic.
I love him so much, which is why I'm emphatic.
RUPERT.
Then put all your worries aside, my sweet niece,
And go and be happy and marry in peace.
The news that I brought you was all a big fake;
It was simply a plan to catch you two a break.
I wanted to prove beyond any small doubt
What a phony dissembler is Gabbitt, that lout.
HENRY.
God be praised — I'm not broke?
PHYLLIS.

                                  Oh, my heart's filled with glee
That Gabbitt will suffer when he comes to see
What a beautiful wedding we'll throw for these two.
HENRY.
(To Dicky.)
I told you you'd marry her, isn't that true?
And to prove that our wealth doesn't make us all snobs,
I'm expanding the business, creating new jobs.
You'll come work with me, Dick. We'll beat this Depression
And give working folk a sense of self-possession.
SYLVIA.
Dicky, I know losing me must be painful,
But I will insist that to Betty you're faithful.
RAMONA.
And me, I suppose, I get left out with nothing.
PHYLLIS.
What, nothing, you say? Hardly! You have your learning;
Philosophy, poetry, art and —
RAMONA.

                          Enough!

MAGDA.
Tomorrow instead of this culture and stuff,
You spend day with me, not with Mother and Aunt,
And I introduce you to a man: Cary Grant.
(Henry kisses Phyllis.)
PHYLLIS.
What's that for?
HENRY.
              That's for you. Put a smile on that face.
Tonight I'm in love with the whole human race!
Judge Arbogast, come, fill the forms like I said.
(To Betty and Dicky.)
The sooner he's finished, the sooner you're wed.
(Ramona switches on the radio. A nifty jazz number. Ramona begins to dance, encouraging the others to join in. Pair by pair, they do: Dicky and Betty, Rupert and Magda, Sylvia and Judge Arbogast. And during all this:)
PHYLLIS.
What? — No! — How — Stop! — Oh my stars! — Are you in a trance?
SYLVIA.
(Dancing.)
I can't help it!
PHYLLIS.
              Henry, no!
HENRY.
(Pulling her to him.)
              Oh shut up and dance!
(Henry and Phyllis join the dance.)

End of Play

PROPERTY LIST

Hatboxes (SYLVIA)
Newspapers (HENRY)
Movie magazines (PHYLLIS)
Canapés (GABBITT)
Drinks (SERVANTS)
Letter (RAMONA)
Small statuette (BETTY)
Letters (RUPERT)
Hat and coat (HENRY)

SOUND EFFECTS

Jazz music on radio
Doorbell

NEW PLAYS

★ **THE EXONERATED by Jessica Blank and Erik Jensen.** Six interwoven stories paint a picture of an American criminal justice system gone horribly wrong and six brave souls who persevered to survive it. "The #1 play of the year…intense and deeply affecting…" *–NY Times*. "Riveting. Simple, honest storytelling that demands reflection." *–A.P.* "Artful and moving…pays tribute to the resilience of human hearts and minds." *–Variety*. "Stark…riveting…cunningly orchestrated." *–The New Yorker*. "Hard-hitting, powerful, and socially relevant." *–Hollywood Reporter*. [7M, 3W] ISBN: 0-8222-1946-8

★ **STRING FEVER by Jacquelyn Reingold.** Lily juggles the big issues: turning forty, artificial insemination and the elusive scientific Theory of Everything in this Off-Broadway comedy hit. "Applies the elusive rules of string theory to the conundrums of one woman's love life. Think *Sex and the City* meets *Copenhagen*." *–NY Times*. "A funny offbeat and touching look at relationships…an appealing romantic comedy populated by oddball characters." *–NY Daily News*. "Where kooky, zany, and madcap meet…whimsically winsome." *–NY Magazine*. "STRING FEVER will have audience members happily stringing along." *–TheaterMania.com*. "Reingold's language is surprising, inventive, and unique." *–nytheatre.com*. "…[a] whimsical comic voice." *–Time Out*. [3M, 3W (doubling)] ISBN: 0-8222-1952-2

★ **DEBBIE DOES DALLAS adapted by Erica Schmidt, composed by Andrew Sherman, conceived by Susan L. Schwartz.** A modern morality tale told as a comic musical of tragic proportions as the classic film is brought to the stage. "A scream! A saucy, tongue-in-cheek romp." *–The New Yorker*. "Hilarious! DEBBIE manages to have it all: beauty, brains and a great sense of humor!" *–Time Out*. "Shamelessly silly, shrewdly self-aware and proud of being naughty. Great fun!" *–NY Times*. "Racy and raucous, a lighthearted, fast-paced thoroughly engaging and hilarious send-up." *–NY Daily News*. [3M, 5W] ISBN: 0-8222-1955-7

★ **THE MYSTERY PLAYS by Roberto Aguirre-Sacasa.** Two interrelated one acts, loosely based on the tradition of the medieval mystery plays. "… stylish, spine-tingling…Mr. Aguirre-Sacasa uses standard tricks of horror stories, borrowing liberally from masters like Kafka, Lovecraft, Hitchcock…But his mastery of the genre is his own…irresistible." *–NY Times*. "Undaunted by the special-effects limitations of theatre, playwright and *Marvel* comic-book writer Roberto Aguirre-Sacasa maps out some creepy twilight zones in THE MYSTERY PLAYS, an engaging, related pair of one acts…The theatre may rarely deliver shocks equivalent to, say, *Dawn of the Dead*, but Aguirre-Sacasa's work is fine compensation." *–Time Out*. [4M, 2W] ISBN: 0-8222-2038-5

★ **THE JOURNALS OF MIHAIL SEBASTIAN by David Auburn.** This epic one-man play spans eight tumultuous years and opens a uniquely personal window on the Romanian Holocaust and the Second World War. "Powerful." *–NY Times*. "[THE JOURNALS OF MIHAIL SEBASTIAN] allows us to glimpse the idiosyncratic effects of that awful history on one intelligent, pragmatic, recognizably real man…" *–NY Newsday*. [3M, 5W] ISBN: 0-8222-2006-7

★ **LIVING OUT by Lisa Loomer.** The story of the complicated relationship between a Salvadoran nanny and the Anglo lawyer she works for. "A stellar new play. Searingly funny." *–The New Yorker*. "Both generous and merciless, equally enjoyable and disturbing." *–NY Newsday*. "A bitingly funny new comedy. The plight of working mothers is explored from two pointedly contrasting perspectives in this sympathetic, sensitive new play." *–Variety*. [2M, 6W] ISBN: 0-8222-1994-8

DRAMATISTS PLAY SERVICE, INC.
440 Park Avenue South, New York, NY 10016 212-683-8960 Fax 212-213-1539
postmaster@dramatists.com   www.dramatists.com

NEW PLAYS

★ **MATCH by Stephen Belber.** Mike and Lisa Davis interview a dancer and choreographer about his life, but it is soon evident that their agenda will either ruin or inspire them—and definitely change their lives forever. "Prolific laughs and ear-to-ear smiles." *–NY Magazine.* "Uproariously funny, deeply moving, enthralling theater. Stephen Belber's MATCH has great beauty and tenderness, and abounds in wit." *–NY Daily News.* "Three and a half out of four stars." *–USA Today.* "A theatrical steeplechase that leads straight from outrageous bitchery to unadorned, heartfelt emotion." *–Wall Street Journal.* [2M, 1W] ISBN: 0-8222-2020-2

★ **HANK WILLIAMS: LOST HIGHWAY by Randal Myler and Mark Harelik.** The story of the beloved and volatile country-music legend Hank Williams, featuring twenty-five of his most unforgettable songs. "[LOST HIGHWAY has] the exhilarating feeling of Williams on stage in a particular place on a particular night…serves up classic country with the edges raw and the energy hot…By the end of the play, you've traveled on a profound emotional journey: LOST HIGHWAY transports its audience and communicates the inspiring message of the beauty and richness of Williams' songs…forceful, clear-eyed, moving, impressive." *–Rolling Stone.* "…honors a very particular musical talent with care and energy… smart, sweet, poignant." *–NY Times.* [7M, 3W] ISBN: 0-8222-1985-9

★ **THE STORY by Tracey Scott Wilson.** An ambitious black newspaper reporter goes against her editor to investigate a murder and finds the *best* story…but at what cost? "A singular new voice…deeply emotional, deeply intellectual, and deeply musical…" *–The New Yorker.* "…a conscientious and absorbing new drama…" *–NY Times.* "…a riveting, tough-minded drama about race, reporting and the truth…" *–A.P.* "… a stylish, attention-holding script that ends on a chilling note that will leave viewers with much to talk about." *–Curtain Up.* [2M, 7W (doubling, flexible casting)] ISBN: 0-8222-1998-0

★ **OUR LADY OF 121st STREET by Stephen Adly Guirgis.** The body of Sister Rose, beloved Harlem nun, has been stolen, reuniting a group of life-challenged childhood friends who square off as they wait for her return. "A scorching and dark new comedy… Mr. Guirgis has one of the finest imaginations for dialogue to come along in years." *–NY Times.* "Stephen Guirgis may be the best playwright in America under forty." *–NY Magazine.* [8M, 4W] ISBN: 0-8222-1965-4

★ **HOLLYWOOD ARMS by Carrie Hamilton and Carol Burnett.** The coming-of-age story of a dreamer who manages to escape her bleak life and follow her romantic ambitions to stardom. Based on Carol Burnett's bestselling autobiography, *One More Time.* "…pure theatre and pure entertainment…" *–Talkin' Broadway.* "…a warm, fuzzy evening of theatre." *–BrodwayBeat.com.* "…chuckles and smiles of recognition or surprise flow naturally…a remarkable slice of life." *–TheatreScene.net.* [5M, 5W, 1 girl] ISBN: 0-8222-1959-X

★ **INVENTING VAN GOGH by Steven Dietz.** A haunting and hallucinatory drama about the making of art, the obsession to create and the fine line that separates truth from myth. "Like a van Gogh painting, Dietz's story is a gorgeous example of excess—one that remakes reality with broad, well-chosen brush strokes. At evening's end, we're left with the author's resounding opinions on art and artifice, and provoked by his constant query into which is greater: van Gogh's art or his violent myth." *–Phoenix New Times.* "Dietz's writing is never simple. It is always brilliant. Shaded, compressed, direct, lucid—he frames his subject with a remarkable understanding of painting as a physical experience." *–Tucson Citizen.* [4M, 1W] ISBN: 0-8222-1954-9

DRAMATISTS PLAY SERVICE, INC.
440 Park Avenue South, New York, NY 10016 212-683-8960 Fax 212-213-1539
postmaster@dramatists.com   www.dramatists.com

NEW PLAYS

★ **INTIMATE APPAREL by Lynn Nottage.** The moving and lyrical story of a turn-of-the-century black seamstress whose gifted hands and sewing machine are the tools she uses to fashion her dreams from the whole cloth of her life's experiences. "…Nottage's play has a delicacy and eloquence that seem absolutely right for the time she is depicting…" *–NY Daily News.* "…thoughtful, affecting…The play offers poignant commentary on an era when the cut and color of one's dress—and of course, skin—determined whom one could and could not marry, sleep with, even talk to in public." *–Variety.* [2M, 4W] ISBN: 0-8222-2009-1

★ **BROOKLYN BOY by Donald Margulies.** A witty and insightful look at what happens to a writer when his novel hits the bestseller list. "The characters are beautifully drawn, the dialogue sparkles…" *–nytheatre.com.* "Few playwrights have the mastery to smartly investigate so much through a laugh-out-loud comedy that combines the vintage subject matter of successful writer-returning-to-ethnic-roots with the familiar mid-life crisis." *–Show Business Weekly.* [4M, 3W] ISBN: 0-8222-2074-1

★ **CROWNS by Regina Taylor.** Hats become a springboard for an exploration of black history and identity in this celebratory musical play. "Taylor pulls off a Hat Trick: She scores thrice, turning CROWNS into an artful amalgamation of oral history, fashion show, and musical theater…" *–TheatreMania.com.* "…wholly theatrical…Ms. Taylor has created a show that seems to arise out of spontaneous combustion, as if a bevy of department-store customers simultaneously decided to stage a revival meeting in the changing room." *–NY Times.* [1M, 6W (2 musicians)] ISBN: 0-8222-1963-8

★ **EXITS AND ENTRANCES by Athol Fugard.** The story of a relationship between a young playwright on the threshold of his career and an aging actor who has reached the end of his. "[Fugard] can say more with a single line than most playwrights convey in an entire script…Paraphrasing the title, it's safe to say this drama, making its memorable entrance into our consciousness, is unlikely to exit as long as a theater exists for exceptional work." *–Variety.* "A thought-provoking, elegant and engrossing new play…" *–Hollywood Reporter.* [2M] ISBN: 0-8222-2041-5

★ **BUG by Tracy Letts.** A thriller featuring a pair of star-crossed lovers in an Oklahoma City motel facing a bug invasion, paranoia, conspiracy theories and twisted psychological motives. "…obscenely exciting…top-flight craftsmanship. Buckle up and brace yourself…" *–NY Times.* "…[a] thoroughly outrageous and thoroughly entertaining play…the possibility of enemies, real and imagined, to squash has never been more theatrical." *–A.P.* [3M, 2W] ISBN: 0-8222-2016-4

★ **THOM PAIN (BASED ON NOTHING) by Will Eno.** An ordinary man muses on childhood, yearning, disappointment and loss, as he draws the audience into his last-ditch plea for empathy and enlightenment. "It's one of those treasured nights in the theater—treasured nights anywhere, for that matter—that can leave you both breathless with exhilaration and…in a puddle of tears." *–NY Times.* "Eno's words…are familiar, but proffered in a way that is constantly contradictory to our expectations. Beckett is certainly among his literary ancestors." *–nytheatre.com.* [1M] ISBN: 0-8222-2076-8

★ **THE LONG CHRISTMAS RIDE HOME by Paula Vogel.** Past, present and future collide on a snowy Christmas Eve for a troubled family of five. "…[a] lovely and hauntingly original family drama…a work that breathes so much life into the theater." *–Time Out.* "…[a] delicate visual feast…" *–NY Times.* "…brutal and lovely…the overall effect is magical." *–NY Newsday.* [3M, 3W] ISBN: 0-8222-2003-2

DRAMATISTS PLAY SERVICE, INC.
440 Park Avenue South, New York, NY 10016   212-683-8960   Fax 212-213-1539
postmaster@dramatists.com   www.dramatists.com